# ILLITERACY IN AMERICA

# ILLITERACY IN AMERICA

Edward F. Dolan and
Margaret M. Scariano

An Impact Book
FRANKLIN WATTS
New York/Chicago/Toronto/London/Sydney

Library of Congress Cataloging-in-Publication Data

Dolan, Edward F., 1924–
Illiteracy in America / Edward F. Dolan and Margaret M. Scariano.
p.     cm. — (An Impact book)
Includes bibliographical references (p.   ) and index.
ISBN 0-531-11178-4
1. Literacy—United States—Juvenile literature.   2. Literacy—
Social aspects—United States—Juvenile literature.   [1. Literacy]
I. Scariano, Margaret M.   II. Title.
LC151.D65   1995
302.2'244'0973—dc20
93-29528   CIP   AC

## ACKNOWLEDGMENTS

The authors wish to thank Reading and Language Arts Specialist Alton L. Greenfield, Ph.D., for his review of their manuscript and his very helpful editorial comments.

# CONTENTS

# ILLITERACY IN AMERICA

# ILLITERACY IN AMERICA

You are very fortunate. You are able to read this book or any other book of your choosing. And, if you wish, you are able to write a book of your own. You are one of the millions of Americans who can read and write. You are, in a word, *literate*.

But suppose that you are not so lucky. Suppose that you are like seventeen-year-old Dan, who lives in northern California. Dan is unable to read or write a letter or look up a number in the telephone directory. A map is useless to him and a contract or job application form is incomprehensible. Traffic or road signs, directions on a medical prescription, or a warning such as DANGER marked on a door are all beyond his understanding.

Dan says, "Sometimes I feel useless—like some dumb bug. And I hate to go to a restaurant. I always have to order a hamburger because I can't read the menu."

Dan is angry, angry that others can read and that somehow the skill has escaped him. Most of all, he is frightened that his secret will be discovered and that he will feel humiliated when everyone knows he can't read.

Dan is what is known as a *total illiterate*. He simply cannot read or write. Being illiterate denies him the opportunity to learn, to know, to communicate, and to be in control of his own life.

While Dan is a total illiterate, there are others like him who are not quite as unfortunate. They are young people who have received some instruction in reading and writing at one time or another. But over the years, for reasons that can vary from individual to individual, they have not used these skills. As a result, their ability to apply them is very limited.

Take for example sixteen-year-old Lora of Chicago. She can read a few words but not enough to read what she really wants to—romance novels. She also wishes she could read the articles on beauty tips in the women's magazines.[1]

People like Lora are said to be *functionally illiterate*. They are able to read and write on a limited level, whereas both are beyond Dan. Because Lora has some literacy skills, she can function better in life than Dan. But she is unable to perform on the same level as those who can read and write well.[2]

Now—and until they learn to read and write—both Dan and Lora are in trouble. Dan will probably be forced to take only menial jobs that do not require reading and writing skills. As a consequence, he may spend his life in low-paying, dead-end jobs.

Lora will also probably have difficulty getting a job that is not menial. Because she cannot fill out a job application form, write a simple business letter, or read memos pertaining to a job, Lora may also have to settle for low-paying, dead-end work.

## TYPES OF ILLITERACY

Total and functional are not the only types of illiteracy found in the United States. Two other types—*cultural* and *professional*—are prevalent in America and elsewhere around the world.[3]

## Cultural Illiteracy

If you are culturally illiterate, you do not know or understand a common body of facts about your nation, your state, or even your hometown. Cultural illiteracy is especially troublesome for newcomers to a country, but it also looms as a great problem for native-born citizens where the lack of literacy skills has kept them from learning as much as they can about where they live.

To see the everyday difficulties that this can cause for the newcomer, put yourself in the position of fourteen-year-old Antonio, who came from Italy with his family in 1985 to live in the United States. During his first years in America, he not only missed his relatives and old friends back in Rome, but he found life puzzling in his new homeland because he did not understand its traditions, its history, and even the figures of speech he heard all around him. He remembers the Saturday morning when he asked his new friend Jim to help him wash the family car, only to hear Jim accuse him of "Tom Sawyering." Antonio was confused and hurt. Not understanding what Jim was talking about, he thought his friend was angry with him. Then Jim told him that he was joking and was referring to a famous scene in the book *Tom Sawyer* by Mark Twain. It's the scene in which Tom tricks his friends into the tiring job of whitewashing the family fence.

As a cultural illiterate, you're in the same boat with Antonio. You experience the same difficulties he faced. You're constantly puzzled by what happens and what is said because you do not yet understand the traditions, the history, the legends, and the everyday figures of speech of your country, with the same holding true for your state, your city, and even your neighborhood.

Worse, knowing little or nothing of national or local history, business life, the arts and literature, and social and political traditions, you lose out on the chance to communicate effectively with the people around you. You are unable to converse with them because you don't know or are uncertain of what they are talking about. It is a basic fact that effective communication is a "must" for successful living. In his book *Cultural Illiteracy*, E. D. Hirsch, Jr., professor of English at the University of Virginia, points out that effective communication demands that the citizens of a society have certain background information if they are to understand what is being said without needing a lengthy explanation of what is meant. Otherwise, impatience, misunderstandings, and even a loss of friends can result.

## Professional Illiteracy

Professional illiteracy concerns the language needed for special kinds of work. Many professions require the use of technical terms to describe various conditions or activities within their field. For instance, a stockbroker talks about stocks, bonds, and mutual funds, while a medical doctor refers to antibiotics and the immune system. If you are professionally illiterate in their fields, you have no idea what the two are talking about.

Kathy, as a new salesperson in a retail computer store, is not knowledgeable about the terms used to describe the various parts and functions of the product she is to sell. When her first customer asks, "How many bytes can this computer handle?" Kathy can only shake her head in confusion. For her, the vocabulary pertaining to the computer is as mystifying as a foreign language. Until she learns the meaning of the myriad computer terms, Kathy will remain professionally illiterate.

On the other hand, Kathy is a talented musician. She is anything but professionally illiterate when it comes to sharps and flats, clefs, and terms such as *pianissimo*.

While a person may be professionally illiterate in one

area, he or she can be far from professionally illiterate in other areas.

## ILLITERACY IN THE UNITED STATES

A little more than 30 percent of the 248.7 million people living in the United States today are said to be totally or functionally illiterate.[4]

According to a 1989 issue of *U.S. News & World Report*, approximately 25 million American adults are reported as totally illiterate; they make up a little more than 10 percent of the nation's population. Some 45 million American adults—almost 20 percent of the nation's population, or one in every five citizens—are known to be functionally illiterate.

In an advanced nation with both a public and private educational system, these statistics are startling and disheartening. But the sad truth is that they tell only part of the story. The United States' illiteracy problem is greater than the figures indicate, due to the fact that the statistics cover only adults and older teenagers. Not included are figures covering younger teenagers and children.

A full picture of the nation's illiterate population is impossible to ascertain because of the methods used by the federal government and other interested organizations to compute when a youngster can be judged to be totally or functionally illiterate. The computations are made on the grounds that children learn at different rates of speed and that they should not be judged illiterate until given the fullest opportunity to master reading and writing. Consequently, young people are usually not listed as totally illiterate until they reach age fifteen. Nor are they judged functionally illiterate until they reveal an inability to read or write as expected at certain grade levels. The International Task Force on Illiteracy, a special group within the United Nations, reports that some organizations designate youngsters as functionally illiterate once they prove themselves unable to read or write at the fifth-grade level. Other organizations postpone a decision until seeing a young person's performance at the completion of the eighth or twelfth grade.

All this being the case, many experts contend that the number of reported total and functional illiterates marks but the "tip of the iceberg" and that the actual total, although unknown, is much greater.

Further, the problem is growing worse. Each year thousands of young Americans reach the age in which they can be added to the number of known functional and total illiterates. Each year sees many non-English-speaking and -writing people settle in the nation. In all, the estimates hold that 2.2 million people, young and old alike, are added to the illiteracy rolls annually.

Where is illiteracy to be found in the United States? The answer is "everywhere." The International Task Force on Illiteracy reports that the problem, both here and abroad, is most often seen among people who are chronically unemployed, in poor health, or living in poverty. But the Task Force quickly points out that illiteracy is found in the nation's affluent population as well.

The problem plagues every one of our ethnic groups. Of the English-speaking white adults in the country, 41 percent are non-literate (meaning that the percentage covers both total and functional illiterates). The rate stands at 22 percent for English-speaking African-Americans and Spanish-speaking Americans, while it is 15 percent for other non-English-speaking people. Of all American adults, some 50 percent are unable to read a book written for eighth-graders.

Wherever you go in the country, you'll encounter illiteracy, whether in rural, suburban, or urban areas. The International Task Force on Illiteracy reports that 51 percent of the nation's illiterates live in small towns and the suburbs, 41 percent are found in urban areas, and 8 percent live in rural regions.

Those who live in rural areas are more fortunate than the others. Various manual and unskilled jobs are available there, and so the illiterate person has a fairly good chance of finding employment and winning social acceptance in the community. The unluckiest ones live in urban and industrialized areas. There they face great and often insurmountable difficulties in making a living because the need for unskilled or manual work is limited. The new technologies employed by industry and business require competence in reading, writing, and computing skills, all of which are beyond the illiterate's capabilities.

There is a connection between illiteracy and the U.S. crime rate. Some 60 percent of the country's prison inmates are functionally or totally illiterate. A staggering 86 percent of American juvenile offenders are known to have reading problems.

In all, the United States, long acknowledged as a world leader in industry and social advances, is far down the list of nations in terms of a literate population. Of the 178 member countries of the United Nations, the United States ranks an embarrassing forty-ninth in its rate of literacy, a drop of eighteen places since 1950.

## ILLITERACY WORLDWIDE

A study completed in 1990 estimates that there are some 965 million illiterates in the world, with 98 percent living in developing and Third World nations.[5] The study also points out that the most densely populated regions of the world, such as Asia and Africa, have the highest concentrations of illiterates. For example, in Asia alone they number around 700 million; 490 million of these are found in China and India. And in the African population

54 percent are illiterate. The most disturbing fact is that in these regions more than 100 million children between six and eleven years of age are not attending school. Unless efforts are quickly and successfully made to educate them, these children will join the ranks of the illiterates by the twenty-first century. By themselves, they will increase the number of the world's illiterates by more than 10 percent.

Most of the world's illiterates are women. Their illiteracy rate worldwide stands at 34.9 percent, as compared to 20.5 percent for men. This percentage, of course, differs from region to region. For example, in such developing nations as Afghanistan, the illiteracy rate for women is 86.1 percent while that for the men is 55.9 percent, a difference of 30 percentage points.

## THE COSTS OF ILLITERACY

*The worker in a Chicago stockyard killed a herd of cattle when he gave them the contents of a bag that he thought contained feed. He could not read the word printed on the bag: POISON.*

*When a female worker in a Los Angeles factory slipped on a floor that had just been washed, she broke her back. Standing at the beginning of the washed area was a warning sign that she was unable to read: CAREFUL—SLIPPERY WHEN WET.*

*A seaman destroyed a quarter of a million dollars' worth of Navy equipment when he tried to install it. He could not read the instruction manual.*

These stories help to demonstrate a major point about illiteracy: It is an expensive problem for a country. It is expensive on three counts—economic, cultural, and political.[6]

## Economic Costs

When employees are illiterate, businesses can easily suffer because of low productivity, industrial accidents, and poor product quality. The low productivity is frequently due to a slowing of work because workers find it impossible to read and comprehend written instructions. Industrial accidents often result from the employees' inability to read simple warning signs. Poor product quality often stems from a lack of pride in their work because, suffering the low self-esteem that almost invariably goes hand in hand with illiteracy, they do not feel themselves capable of doing a good job. All these factors cost the United States more than $20 billion a year in diminished productivity, lost tax revenues, disability benefits that must be paid in the event of injury, and welfare payments made to the illiterates who are unemployable.

In addition, another $5 billion is lost annually in tax money that goes to support public-assistance programs for unemployable illiterates.

The United States is not alone in paying a high price for illiteracy. The economic costs borne by other countries are just as alarmingly high—even more so for those countries not as wealthy as we are. Exact figures on the cost of illiteracy worldwide are not available, but one expert in the field remarks that they have been calculated to be "enormous." Considering the amount that the United States alone spends on the problem, the annual global costs obviously run into the trillions of dollars.

## Cultural Costs

The costs to a society's culture are great because illiteracy throws up a wall between the individual and the nation's print media. He or she is cut off from the enjoyment and vital information to be discovered in books, magazines, and newspapers and, as a consequence, is unable to participate fully in the civic, social, cultural, and educational activities that surround us all and enrich our lives.

Lost to the community, the state, and the nation are the contributions that the illiterate could make for his or her own well-being and betterment if only he or she could read or write.

## Political Costs

Finally, there are the terrible political costs. Illiterate people, especially those who are totally so, are too often helpless to understand and voice their rights as citizens. If their number is great enough, they can be powerless to stop their nation from falling into the hands of an oppressive or unstable government. As a case in point, take the country of Guatemala, located in the northern part of Central America. With a population of 9.4 million, of whom 62 percent are illiterate, Guatemala has been directly or indirectly under military rule since 1954. Since 1960, it has suffered economically because political violence by antigovernment guerrillas has caused more than 200,000 Guatemalans—among them literate doctors, lawyers, teachers, and business leaders who could contribute to the nation's industry and economy—to seek refuge in Mexico.

The United Nations Educational, Scientific, and Cultural Organization (UNESCO) has long been dedicated to ending illiteracy worldwide. In June 1989, UNESCO issued an informational publication titled *1990: International Literacy Year.* (There is more information on the International Literacy Year in a later chapter.) In the publication, the organization stated that the work of ending global illiteracy—both total and functional—stands before us all as a challenge and an opportunity. The challenge is to discover ways to overcome illiteracy everywhere. The opportunity is to raise the self-esteem and dignity of illiterate people everywhere by opening the door to their personal development and the development of their countries.[7]

The purpose of this book is to speak of the dangers that illiteracy poses for us all, and to talk of the challenge and opportunity that it offers anyone who wishes to help end it here and throughout the world. To achieve this purpose, the coming chapters will look into the following topics:

*The reasons total and functional illiteracy have gained such a foothold in the United States.*

*The reasons women have long suffered a higher illiteracy rate than men, not only in foreign nations but in the United States.*

*The steps being taken in the United States and worldwide to end the tragedy that is illiteracy.*

Finally, and perhaps most important of all, we'll talk of what you can do at present as a concerned young person—and later as an adult—to assist in putting an end to this tragedy.

Before we can look into any of these topics, however, we need to talk about the history of illiteracy in America so that we can gain a greater understanding of how it came to be such a problem for our country. With this understanding, we will be in a better position to see what can, and must, be done to end what many of our citizens are calling a national disgrace.

# THE RISE AND FALL OF LITERACY IN THE UNITED STATES

The story of illiteracy in America is one that forms a circle. It begins with settlers whose numbers included thousands who could neither read nor write and saw no value in learning to do so. It then advances to decades when attitudes slowly changed and the skills of literacy became highly prized throughout the nation. They were years that saw the United States achieve one of the lowest illiteracy rates in the world. Finally, it covers a time that brings us up to the present—a time when illiteracy again began to rise and eventually became the national tragedy that it is today.

## ILLITERACY IN EARLY AMERICA

Our story begins in the seventeenth century, when the Pilgrims and the Puritans established two settlements in what is now the state of Massachusetts, the Pilgrims at Plymouth in 1620, and the Puritans at Salem in 1628.[1]

Both were peoples who, because of their religious zeal, greatly admired the skills of reading and writing. They had learned to read so that they could study the Bible and thus better serve God and oppose Satan. Consequently, their literacy rate was high; actually, to put it correctly, it was *high among the men.* For reasons we'll discuss later, the women were not expected to read, and so most of their number were illiterate. This was a misfortune that was to dog women everywhere in the New World for years to come.

Great numbers of settlers left Europe and sailed westward to America in the wake of the Pilgrims and Puritans. Coming from such countries as England, Germany, Norway, and the Netherlands, they not only settled along the Atlantic coast but also ventured into the vast interior. Many of the newcomers could read and write, but, unfortunately, a greater number were illiterate. The illiterates came mostly from farming regions where reading and writing were considered of little value. These people had always felt there were more important things to do. They had to work their farms. They had to tend their animals. They had to raise enough crops to feed their families.

In brief, they had to survive. For them, experience with and knowledge of the land—not the niceties of reading and writing—were what counted. They brought this attitude to the New World and then passed it on to their children who were born here.

But, remember, this is not to say that every newcomer was illiterate. Among the settlers who joined the Puritans in what is now being called New England were people of other religious denominations. Like the Puritans, and for the same reasons, they put great stock in the ability to read and write. They founded schools for their children—specifically, their boys—with the teachers often being the ministers of their churches. Competition was keen among the schools of the various denominations. Each wanted its young males to be the best educated of all in religious subjects and in the ability to read the Bible.

Along with establishing these schools, the religious denominations, including the Puritans, founded America's first three universities: Harvard (Massachusetts) in 1636, just sixteen years after Plymouth got its start; William and Mary (Virginia) in 1693; and Yale (Connecticut) in 1701. At the time of their foundings, the chief aim of the three, and those that followed them in the next years, was to prepare young men for the ministry.

But what of the others in the literate classes—the merchants, the professionals, and the wealthy—whose sons did not wish to become ministers? In the South of the late 1600s and early 1700s, where universities had yet to be founded, the wealthy plantation owners hired tutors to educate their sons. They then either sent the youths off to college in Europe or enrolled them in an American university to take advantage of the few courses that were not meant solely for future clerics. Southern girls, as was the case far to the north in New England, were trained by their mothers for the task of maintaining a household. The black slaves, who first arrived in the South in 1609 and were now being used there to work the rice and tobacco fields, received no education at all.

Young people who did not wish to become ministers but instead planned to enter a trade or a profession turned to a different type of education. They trained for their future work by means of what was called the apprenticeship system. The apprenticeship system was limited to young men because women were years away from being admitted to the workplace. The system called for a young man to take instruction from someone experienced in a given field. If the apprentice wished to become a doctor, he worked with a physician and followed him on his rounds among the sick. The young man who hoped to be a lawyer was taken under the wing of a practicing attorney. The same held true for youths who planned to become retail merchants, shoemakers, blacksmiths, or furniture makers.

Some of the trades and all of the professions required the apprentice to be literate. If he had only a rudimentary skill in reading and writing, he devoted a share of his time to developing that skill.

## THE BEGINNINGS OF A
## SCHOOL SYSTEM IN AMERICA

The first American schools for young children were, as you know, those sponsored by the different religious denominations.[2] But not all the towns along the Atlantic coast and to the interior were blessed with such schools. And so, in what had become the Massachusetts Bay Colony (the area fanning out for miles around Salem), an effort was made to ensure that all its towns would build schools. On November 11, 1647, the colonial legislature enacted a law that required every town with more than fifty families to establish and support an elementary school to teach reading, writing, and arithmetic. Towns with 100 families or more were also to establish a secondary school in which boys prepared to enter a university and study for the ministry.

Records indicate that only a few towns obeyed this law. Many, especially those in distant rural areas, were made up of farmers who had brought to the New World the tradition of seeing little value in reading and writing. Further, as had been their lot back home, they found that the rigors of working their farms in the harsh countryside consumed all their energies, and those of their children, who, as soon as they were old enough, had to share in the work. The youngsters had little or no time left for a proper education.

The Massachusetts act marked the first effort to provide America with a public school system. But it was a system exactly opposite to the one found in the United

States today. Unlike today's system, it was not financed by public moneys. Rather, the towns had to bear the costs of building their schools and paying their teachers. Some towns were fortunate enough to have wealthy citizens who supported the schools through donations. In some towns, parents paid a tuition, with the amount based on the number of children they sent to class. And in some towns, the wealthy established schools for their children. In all, then, only people who could afford it were able to take advantage of a local school. The poor were denied the same advantage.

This situation persisted for decades, until the United States was established in the wake of the Revolutionary War. The next steps toward the formation of a public school system came in the 1780s, when the Congress of the Confederation (a legislative body made up of representatives of the thirteen original states; Congress as we know it today had yet to be formed) enacted two ordinances, the Land Ordinance of 1785 and the Northwest Ordinance of 1787. These ordinances stated that every township formed in the Northwest Territory—all the land that lay north of the Ohio River—was to set aside 1 square mile for the establishment of a "school lot" for building a school and a "gospel lot" to be used for a church.

The nation's new Constitution, however, included no mention of public education, so the people could not be forced to obey the two acts. Rather, the decision to set aside the land was left to the individual communities.

## The One-Room Schoolhouses

Because of the acts and because a growing number of settlers now wanted to see their children, both boys and girls, educated so that the youngsters would have brighter futures, the communities that took shape on the ever-advancing western frontier began establishing what came to be called one-room schoolhouses.

The one-room schoolhouse, which was all that a rural village could afford, was usually constructed of logs and had a roof of rough-hewn shingles. Here, children of various ages, usually from six to well into their teens, sat together at long tables and were taught by a single teacher. For much of the time, the teacher worked with individual students while the others studied their textbooks or wrote assignments on small chalkboards called slates. While the little ones, for instance, were learning to spell simple words, the older pupils would be writing longer words or doing arithmetic problems on their slates.

Life for the children who attended the one-room schoolhouse was anything but easy. Often, they had to walk or ride a horse for miles to attend class. If they had to go to the toilet, they walked across the schoolyard, often in harsh winter weather, to an outhouse. If they wanted a drink of water, they went to a common pail. Their only warmth came from a fireplace or wood stove that occupied one corner of the classroom. It was customary for parents, in addition to the small fee they paid for educating their children, to provide wood for the fire. If a father neglected to bring in his share of the wood, his shivering child sat farthest from the warmth. On top of all else, discipline was firm and punishment for misbehavior or inattention swift. A row of hickory sticks, used for what was called "humbling," always stood alongside the teacher's desk, ready to smack a backside or the palm of an upturned hand.

Very often, the education given the children was not especially good. Many of the teachers knew little beyond what was contained in the simple books—the spelling, grammar, penmanship, reading, and arithmetic books— that were used as texts. Yet, from the late 1700s to our own twentieth century, countless American boys and girls went on to successful and productive lives after a childhood in the one-room schoolhouse. Among them was Abraham Lincoln, who attended a one-room school for a year; his daily walk to and from class added up to eighteen miles.

## THE NINETEENTH CENTURY

In the late 1800s, Americans recognized the need for all of the nation's people to receive an education if they were to serve as responsible citizens in a democracy and help the country to prosper.[3] They believed that the cost of public education should be financed by taxation and not by the fees that until then had been charged. After all, the United States was becoming more industrialized and it was obvious that workers needed to know how to read and write. More sophisticated machinery required that written instructions be read; orders for parts be filled out; memos from supervisors be understood.

To achieve the goal of an education for all the nation's children, a system of what were called common schools was established. Three principles guided its formation. First, despite the various languages and customs that newcomers from the world over were bringing into the country, there was the principle that the system would succeed only if it taught a common language and a common appreciation of U.S. citizenship. This idea was fostered by such educational statesmen as Horace Mann in Massachusetts and Robert Breckinridge in Kentucky.

Next, so that the same opportunities would be available to all—not just the wealthy—there was the principle that everyone must have an equal chance to attend school; this made it necessary to have a system that was financed by taxation. Finally, because America was being settled by people of many different religious affiliations, there was the principle that the public schools must not be influenced by any given religious organization and must not teach any given religious belief.

By the end of the nineteenth century, most states had

free public elementary schools, with the one-room schoolhouses of old becoming part of the free system in many areas. The new system did not call for compulsory classroom attendance. In many states, the school term lasted only twelve weeks a year, in great part so that the children would have more time to help at home on the farm, especially during harvest times.

## Technical Improvements in Printing
Between 1800 and 1900, technical improvements in printing, such as steel engravings and mechanical presses, made it possible to produce many more books, newspapers, and magazines. The availability of more reading material served to increase the literacy rate.

## Immigrants
Prior to 1875, people from any foreign country could enter the United States to live here. Between 1845 and 1855, immigration from Europe greatly increased, rising from around 84,000 annually to no less than 300,000 a year. Accounting chiefly for the increase were widespread unemployment in England, the potato famine in Ireland, and raging political unrest in Germany. The English and German immigrants settled mainly on farms, while the Irish newcomers preferred the cities and obtained public service jobs such as policemen or firemen. But in time all were generally assimilated into the American culture.

Immigration after 1890 saw the arrival of many newcomers from southern and eastern Europe, people from Italy, Greece, Poland, and Russia who were fleeing their homelands because of famine, lack of social and economic opportunities, or political or religious persecution. These immigrants were not farmers and they tended to remain in cities to work in coal and mineral mines, steel mills, and textile factories. They lived among their own people and did not adopt American customs or even obey American laws. Immigrant aid societies, such as New York's Shamrock Society, were organized to help them adjust to life in the United States.

A problem caused by many of the new arrivals was greatly responsible for the next major step in the nation's public school system. The states began passing laws that demanded compulsory classroom attendance by youngsters from age seven through fourteen. In great part, the states called for these measures because so many immigrant children were roaming the streets and causing trouble. The laws were also aimed at keeping the children from going to work and taking jobs from adults by laboring for lower wages.

Beginning in the mid-nineteenth century, various groups of Americans wanted to curb the flow of immigration. Some groups said that limiting the influx of foreigners was an economic necessity because the newcomers worked for less money and thus "stole" jobs from U.S. citizens. The ugly hand of prejudice was also seen: Many groups disliked those whose skin color, traditions, and religious beliefs differed from their own. And many argued that the immigrants were at fault for a rising crime rate.

Responding to these views, Congress enacted anti-immigration laws in 1862 and 1875. They prohibited the importation of prostitutes, convicts, and Asian slave laborers. Further enactments between 1882 and 1907 tightened the immigration restrictions to include the mentally ill, epileptics, paupers, polygamists, individuals with contagious diseases, and aliens convicted of crimes involving moral misconduct.

Between 1896 and 1906, several bills aimed at reducing the flow of immigrants by requiring them to pass a literacy test before being allowed into the country were proposed to Congress. The legislators defeated these bills on the grounds that they would cut off a labor force needed by the growing U.S. economy and would prohibit many deserving families from entering the nation to enjoy its freedoms. However, in 1915 Congress approved a bill requiring literacy for admission to the United States, only to have President Woodrow Wilson veto it because he said that the ability to read "was not a test of character, of quality or of personal fitness." In 1917, Congress overrode Mr. Wilson's veto and enacted the nation's first literacy act. It required aliens over sixteen years of age to be able to read between thirty and eighty English words.

From the establishment of America's first colonies up until the nineteenth century, two groups were ignored as far as literacy was concerned—women and blacks. During the nineteenth century attention was given to the literacy needs of both. Women were the first of the two to receive this attention.

## Education for Women

During the colonial period, more than half the women in the United States were illiterate because their ability to read or write was thought to be of no consequence. Why? Every woman was legally considered the property of her husband, who had complete authority over her and her possessions. As such, any wages she might earn belonged to her spouse. In the rare event that a document required her signature, she could sign it with an X and it would be perfectly legal. Consequently, the prevailing attitude was that, since she could make no legal and business decisions on her own, there was no need for her to be literate and educated.

This does not mean, however, that she went without any education at all. Young women from wealthy families often received instruction in the fashionable language, French, and in such "ladylike arts" as painting, music, and dancing. But, in general, the girls of the time married young, and their education was limited to learning from their mothers such practical household chores as cooking, sewing, soap making, and candle dipping.

For almost 200 years, most girls received no formal education. A fortunate few, usually those from more enlightened families, were sent to what were called *dame schools*. Such schools were located in private homes and were run by housewives who taught very young children the alphabet and other educational fundamentals for a small fee. But, in addition to the feeling that there was no need to educate a woman, it was widely believed (by most men and some women) that the female mind was so fragile that to tax it with learning could trigger disaster. This belief was supported by a rumor heard for many years that a colonial governor's wife had lost her wits from thinking and reading too much.

A number of enlightened people disagreed with the idea that women should not be educated. Among them was the highly respected physician and thinker, Dr. Benjamin Rush (1746–1813). In 1787, in his book *Thoughts on Female Education*, he wrote that if the United States was to have educated children, it must have educated mothers. Unfortunately, few Americans shared his belief.

Girls, however, had always been welcome in the one-room schoolhouses out on the frontier. Later, after the birth of the common school system, they were gradually allowed to attend the first public elementary schools. However, unlike the girls in the one-room schoolhouses, they were not allowed to attend regular classes. They could go to class only before and after the regular school day. And they were not permitted, as had been the case since the first days of colonization, to attend secondary and college classes.

The latter part of the nineteenth century saw the number of the nation's elementary and high schools steadily increase. Suddenly, two reasons for educating women became apparent: they were needed as trained teachers in all the new schools and they could be paid less than a man. From the 1890s through the early 1900s, women teachers in city schools averaged $13 a week while their male counterparts earned two or three times that amount.

This discrepancy in men and women teachers' salaries existed for many years.

The need for women teachers spurred the founding of many private schools for girls. Although some of the schools still stressed dancing, music, French, and the social amenities as proper subjects for young ladies, a few, such as Emma Willard's Female Seminary in New York and Catharine Beecher's school in Connecticut, taught more than just the social graces. To justify education for women, these schools emphasized the domestic applications of the subjects they taught. For instance, chemistry could be applied to cooking, and mathematics could improve a woman's ability to keep her household accounts. Not long after the Civil War, women were also allowed to attend the state universities.

**Education for Blacks**
The end of the Civil War gave millions of slaves their freedom. Though liberated, they were uneducated and, of equal importance, unaccustomed to providing their own food and clothing because their former masters had always furnished them with such necessities. The Freedmen's Bureau, an organization formed to ensure the rights of the former slaves, along with missionary societies from various northern churches, went into the South to help them adjust to their new freedom. The bureau and the societies provided food, clothing, fuel, and hospital care to a large number of former slaves. The bureau and the societies also put a strong emphasis on education. They gathered blacks of all ages in church basements and storefronts and instructed them in reading and writing.

When the Freedmen's Bureau ended its work in the early 1870s, 21 percent of all southern blacks could read. Some 4,000 schools had been established, including a dozen colleges exclusively for blacks. Among that dozen were Fisk University in Tennessee, Hampton Institute in Virginia, and Alabama's Tuskegee Institute.

But white southerners, not wanting any traffic with

the former slaves, soon passed segregation laws dictating that educational facilities for blacks and whites were to be separate but equal. For many years, the facilities remained separate but were a far cry from equal. Each year, the public moneys allocated to education favored the white schools. The black schools chronically suffered a lack of funds to maintain their facilities, purchase equipment, and employ needed teachers.

## THE TWENTIETH CENTURY

By 1880, the U.S. illiteracy rate stood at 17 percent in a total population of close to 51 million. Much had been done since colonial times to bring the skills of reading and writing to greater and greater numbers of people. Now, marked by an increasing number of public and private schools and by the interest of families in education, the remaining decades of the 1800s and then the first half of the twentieth century recorded an even greater accomplishment—the almost complete elimination of illiteracy in the country.[4]

The advance toward this triumph could be seen at the end of each ten-year period, when the U.S. Bureau of the Census took a head count of the nation's people. The bureau did so by submitting a questionnaire to all households. One of the questions asked was: Can the people in the household read and write? The answer left no doubt that the illiteracy rate was steadily spiraling downward.

By 1890, for example, the U.S. population numbered 62.9 million, but the illiteracy rate had dropped more than 3 percentage points to 13.3 percent. By 1910, the population had reached 91.9 million, with the illiteracy rate shrinking to 7.7 percent. Twenty years later, in 1930, the population hit the 123.2 million mark; the illiteracy rate had plunged to 4.3 percent. The rate continued to drop for another two decades until, in 1950, it was estimated to be at an all-time low: a mere 3.2 percent in a population numbering 151.3 million.

(The Bureau of the Census, thinking that most Americans were literate in the 1940s, dropped the inquiry about reading and writing from its questionnaire for a number of years. In 1970, the question was put back in place, but was rephrased. Instead of asking whether citizens can read and write, the bureau asks how many years of schooling they have. It then tries to compute the illiteracy rate on the basis of the answers and on the results of a telephone survey it conducts with a small sampling of people.)

The picture at the end of the 1950 census was a rosy one. The United States could boast that it ranked among the world's most literate nations. But suddenly there were indications that the picture was really not so rosy after all.

Actually, the first hints that trouble loomed on the horizon came during World Wars I and II. In both conflicts, the U.S. Army reported that it was being forced to reject many young men for service because they were unable to understand the kinds of written instructions necessary for carrying out basic military tasks. This news came as a shock, especially during World War II, because more service people were found to be illiterate than in the earlier conflict. (This was to be expected, because 16 million Americans served in the armed forces during World War II, as compared to 4 million in 1917–1918.) The shock ballooned in the years following the coming of peace in 1945, as business and industry began reporting that increasing numbers of young Americans were unable to read instructions, comprehend test questions, and write simple communications.

The military went on complaining. In the 1980s, the Navy said flatly that 30 percent of its young recruits were "a danger to themselves and to costly naval equipment" because they were unable to read and comprehend instructions. Remember the story of the young sailor who destroyed some $250,000 worth of equipment because of his inability to read the accompanying instruction manual? He had tried to figure out how the equipment worked by checking the pictures in the manual.

Throughout the 1980s, business, industrial, and military leaders all charged that the accelerating decline in literacy was costing them millions of dollars annually in remedial and educational programs to provide employees and recruits with the basic skills of reading, writing, spelling, and computation.

The states joined the outcry. The Bureau of the Census reported in 1976 that the number of Americans with high school diplomas had doubled since that banner year of 1950. But there was the widespread understanding that a high school diploma no longer guaranteed competence in reading and writing; too many seniors were graduating without the ability to do either. And so, during the late 1980s and into the early 1990s, a number of states established laws requiring high school students to pass a comprehensive literacy test before being permitted to graduate.

The early 1990s have brought more bad news. A survey taken by the Louis Harris polling organization has revealed that employers must reject five out of every six young job applicants because the applicants cannot fill out application forms, fail to write legibly on the forms, or fail to pass the company's standard reading and mathematical tests.

All the complaints have triggered a question asked by countless troubled Americans. Why has the inability to read and write spread to millions of our citizens in the four decades since the country could boast its all-time low illiteracy rate of 3.2 percent? For possible answers, we turn to our next chapter.

# Why Illiteracy: Classrooms and Conveniences

When asked why total and functional illiteracy now have such a grip on the country, Americans reply with a variety of reasons, reasons that range from the way reading is taught in the modern classroom to a number of social factors troubling the United States today. They add, however, that no one reason alone is to blame for the problem. Rather, the fault lies with a combination of factors.

One such combination ranks particularly high in the minds of most Americans. It involves the classroom instruction given in reading (and many other subjects) and the electronic conveniences—chief among them television—that today are not only interfering with reading but are also blunting our various other thinking skills.

## THE CLASSROOM

Experts generally agree that, oddly enough, the start of today's problem can be traced back to a time when the illiteracy rate was plunging, to 1929, the year of the stock market crash.[1] The crash opened the way to the Great Depression of the 1930s, an era in which millions of people lost their jobs, their savings, their homes. It was a period of scarce money and high unemployment that had tragic consequences not only for the general public but for the nation's public schools as well.

The schools' budgets were slashed to the bone. Many schools fell into disrepair, and thousands were forced to close their doors. Countless teachers endured salary cuts while the most unfortunate lost their jobs. Those still lucky enough to be employed took on larger and larger classes, which resulted in less and less individual attention for the students. The whole situation could not help but cause the teaching of reading and writing to suffer.

The damage being done to reading and writing did not, however, disappear when the United States entered World War II in the early 1940s and put an end to the depression by creating millions of jobs in the nation's defense industry. In the minds of many Americans— including many educators—the damage continued during the war and has continued ever since. Said to be at fault are several factors, the first of which dates back to the years immediately following the return of peace.

Those years were nicknamed the "baby boom" years because of the number of children born to the families of veterans returning home from the fighting. Between 1942 and 1950, 30 million children were born. These youngsters began crowding into the nation's classrooms in the early 1950s, creating a desperate need for teachers. To meet the need, millions of young American men and women enrolled in universities and prepared for careers in education. In time, many veteran educators and large segments of the public came to believe that the overwhelming demand for teachers had opened the door to many newcomers who were really not suited for the work, and that the quality of U.S. education—including the quality of reading and writing instruction—was suffering as a consequence.

Another factor that was, and still is, much blamed for the decline in literacy skills is the approach to teaching called "progressive education." This approach is based on the idea that students be allowed to express themselves freely. It encourages children to be taught through activities rather than by rote learning, or learning through repetitious exercises and memorization, which had long been employed for such subjects as reading, writing, and spelling. Actually, progressive education has been part of American education since the late 1800s, but it came to full flower during the years immediately following World War II. Since then, as we'll soon see, it has been widely criticized for not demanding disciplined work from students. Critics of the system contend that the lack of discipline is greatly to blame for the slump in literacy skills.

Still another factor that has earned much blame is the fact that progressive education uses what is called the "whole-word" method of teaching reading. It differs greatly from the "phonics" method of reading instruction used in earlier years. To see the difference, we need to compare the two systems.

Were you to learn to read by the phonics approach, the teacher would first acquaint you with the individual sounds you make when speaking. Then you would be shown the letter or combinations of letters that represent each of these sounds. From that start, you would learn how to read and write these letters singly and in their various combinations.

To give two very simple examples, you would combine the sound *ca* with the sound made by *t* to come up with *cat*. The same would be done by combining the sounds made by *b* and *oy* to figure out the word *boy*. From such simple combinations as these, you would go on to identify new and more complicated words.

In contrast, the whole-word method, in general,

encourages you to memorize an entire word and then gradually build up the number of words you can recognize. The method calls for you to begin your instruction by studying what are known as pre-reader books. These books have no words but contain pictures of the fictional characters and pets you will read about when you open your first book with words. This picture introduction is described as "reading readiness" because it is preparing you for the words that are soon to come. The words arrive when you are given a slender reader with many pictures and a story made up of simple words such as *look, see, oh, run, mother, Jane, Spot.* Pictures throughout the book show the characters and their actions. Next you move on to new books, all of which contain new words.

Behind the whole-word method is the theory that each word is the symbol of an idea and that words can be recognized by their appearance.

Many people criticize the whole-word method for ignoring the phonics approach of mastering words through learning their individual parts. This is a mistaken criticism. The whole-word method does not ignore phonics completely, but puts it to use in a certain way. It calls on phonics to help you build new words on words that you've already learned. For example, suppose that you've learned the words *bread* and *town.* You can now be taught a new word by analyzing how the *br* in *bread* and the *own* in *town* can be joined to come up with *brown.*

Despite its use of phonics, the whole-word method has been widely condemned as confusing for students. A principal complaint has been that it leaves the student unable to distinguish between words on the basis of their length and the combination of letters in them. A California woman has complained, "One of the first words my son learned was *mother.* After that—until I started to coach him myself—he thought that all words that began with *m* were *mother.* It didn't matter what letters were in them or how long or short they were in length—*men, Mary, mama, Mickey*, and *Minnie Mouse*—they were all *mother* when they started with an *m*. No one had made him aware of the letters that followed it."

Her complaint is echoed by a mother in the Midwest: "My son couldn't see the difference between such words as *ant, and, can*, or *cat*, and *when, what*, or *where*." She goes on to·speak of what happened to her daughter. "In one of her first readers, Susan was shown a picture of a girl with the word *Jane* under it. From then on, whenever she came upon the picture of a girl or a woman, that person was Jane."

In great part, the phonics method lost favor among progressive educators from the very beginning because it was taught through rote memorization and, as a consequence, was thought to be boring. Today, a growing number of educators direct the same criticism at the whole-word method. They argue that the reading time in many elementary schools is devoted to dull word-drill workbooks and readers, such as the See Jane Run series, that fail to exercise and excite the child's mind. Among those who hold this view are Robert Barnes and Jim Cates. Barnes is an official with the U.S. Department of Education; Cates is a researcher with the University of Texas. Both contend that the whole-word method is at least partly to blame for the increase in the nation's illiteracy rate.

John Silber, the president of Boston University, attacks the entire approach to reading and writing instruction in the early grades. In his book, *Shooting Straight: What's Wrong with America and How to Fix It*, he draws a comparison between the ideals of modern progressive education and those of earlier times. Saying that progressive educators, like many parents, have long sought to turn out "happy" and "well-balanced" children, he writes that eighteenth- and nineteenth-century parents or teachers never thought that it was their duty to be a "pal" to their children. Nor did they think that it was their duty to make life easy, pleasurable, and comfortable for the youngsters. Rather, they felt it was their responsibility to prepare the children for the uncertainty, harsh realities, and responsibilities that life holds for everyone.

To perform that duty, pre-progressive education was built around texts and workbooks containing not simple stories of Jane and Spot but ideas that challenged and expanded the young mind. To show what very young students were once required to do, Dr. Silber points to an early writing workbook, *The Art of Penmanship.* Each lesson in the workbook was headed by a saying, one of which was *Persevere in accomplishing a complete education.* The youngsters were made to copy the sentence a number of times, even though they were just beginning to learn to write and were unfamiliar with the words. The copying went on until the axiom was learned by heart. Silber maintains that a multi-faceted lesson was learned. The students came to know both the simple and complex words; they came to understand the importance of the saying so that they could apply it in later life; and they learned the art of perseverance through the very act of writing the sentence again and again.

Other sayings that headed the pages in the writing workbooks of the day included:

> *Quarrelsome persons are always dangerous*
> *    companions.*
> *Praise follows exertion.*
> *Overcome all prejudice.*
> *Zeal for justice is worthy of praise.*

Dr. Silber argues that young children are fascinated by "grown-up words" and ideas and by the "attraction and power of language." Implicit in what he writes is the belief that the mind is exactly like a muscle. If the muscle is exercised and worked, it grows strong. If not, it weakens. The mind likewise grows strong if challenged and made to reach out to grasp words and ideas that may seem to be beyond its reach at a given age, especially a very young age. A failure to do so always sees it grow weak and lazy.

When considering the criticisms that have been leveled against progressive education and its whole-word method of instruction, it must be remembered that neither has been a complete failure. Over the years, America's system of modern education has turned out countless literate students who have gone on to live successful and productive lives and have contributed much to the advancement of the nation. Further, if, as charged, the whole-word system itself is responsible for today's widespread illiteracy, it is only *partly* responsible. Other factors are contributing to the illiteracy problem.

For example, teachers complain of today's crowded classrooms and the strain that the crowding puts on all learning. They argue that, with so many children in their care, they have neither the time nor the opportunity to provide the individual attention required by the student with a reading problem. They add that the schools need more funding to reduce class sizes and provide the texts, equipment, special teachers, and individual instruction necessary to improve reading and writing skills. Finally, they point to technological developments that have taken shape outside the schools since World War II and that, despite the good that they have done, have had an unhappy effect on classroom work and learning—namely, the miracles that have emerged from the science of electronics.

## THE ELECTRONIC AGE

Ever since the end of World War II in 1945, daily life in America's homes and classrooms has undergone major changes because of the advances made in electronic technology.[2] The invention of television is just one such advance—but one of the mightiest.

Many educators, and great segments of the American public, believe that television is much to blame for the spread of illiteracy. Since its debut on the national scene in the late 1940s, TV has provided hours of companionship, entertainment, and information for millions of families. But, for countless families, it has replaced newspapers, magazines, and books as the chief source of information and entertainment. The replacement has eroded the reading habit in many literate adults and has contributed to the spread of illiteracy among America's young.

All this has occurred because television is so easy to switch on and then sit back and watch. Reading, however, is a disciplined act, even for accomplished readers; it requires the mental effort to turn combinations of letters into words and then see how those words form themselves into thoughts. Television simply does not call for the same effort. Consequently, many adults have preferred the ease of watching and listening to the trouble of working their way down the printed page. And many students, on learning the basics of reading, have not bothered to go on from there, but have been lured to the effortless task of watching TV's pictures.

Further, television is accused of shortening a person's attention span. Viewers have become programmed to interruptions every ten to fifteen minutes for commercial "messages," a pretty term for advertisements. In addition, television has developed the technique of short visual scenes; they move swiftly from one to the other, providing us with a succession of colorful and fast-changing images. Both the interruptions and the rapid-fire scenes are said to have done two great harms to our reading skills. For one, they have blunted our imagination, an imagination that is called into play when, while reading a book, we transform the description of characters and places into people and places we can actually see in our mind's eye. For the other, they have made us impatient for change, an impatience that has dulled or even ended our interest in the slower act of reading.

In taking us away from printed material, television is accused of damaging us on still another count. According to journalist Pico Iyer, in *Time* magazine, it fails to differentiate between information and real wisdom. In his essay, "History? Education? Zap! Pow! Cut!," he writes that TV customarily bombards us with information rather than knowledge. The two are quite different, with the former often made up of random and miscellaneous facts that do not lead us to firm conclusions, while the latter consists of insights and understandings that we accumulate over a period of time. Iyer contends that TV's constant bombardments of informational messages eventually overwhelm our consciousness and damage the depth of our understanding. That depth is best attained through reading, because a book, a magazine article, or a newspaper report can go more deeply into a subject than can the usual television program. Further, when reading, we have the time to stop and think about what the writer has said and to add our own thoughts to it; in this way, we help ourselves gather knowledge. Television does not grant us this privilege. As soon as it has said one thing to us, it moves on to the next.

But all this is not to say that television does not have its good side. There is no doubt that it can bring knowledge as well as information as we sit watching it at home or in the classroom. It has already done so on a number of occasions, as anyone who has seen the documentary series, "The Civil War," will agree. Produced by Ken Burns, "The Civil War" was first presented nationwide in the early 1990s and has been often aired since. Another example of TV's good side comes from Michael Griest, a high school social studies teacher in Peekskill, New York. He recently tried Cable News Network's

"CNN Newsroom" in his class and found that it added much to his students' understanding of world and national events.

For several decades now, television has been beamed into the nation's classrooms and homes for a variety of educational purposes. In the classroom, in addition to providing young people with daily news coverage, it has been used successfully to depict scientific and mathematical concepts, to instruct in art, to discuss literary works, and to re-create historic events. In both the classroom and the home, it has coached viewers in subjects that are needed on the job market or in daily life—subjects that include typing, shorthand, the writing of business letters, reading improvement, and foreign languages.

All this has been of great value to young and old alike. But a sharp warning comes from Dr. Dorothy Singer of the Department of Psychology at Yale University: Television can *supplement* the material found in a book. But it *cannot be a substitute* for a book.

While television has been one of the most significant of the electronic developments, its significance is matched and even surpassed by another technological miracle—the computer. Able to perform a wide variety of tasks, it has been called the "super electronic device of the century." Its services range from solving mathematical problems, creating three-dimensional figures, and producing graphs to listing word synonyms and correcting grammar and spelling mistakes.

But in the eyes of many of its critics, it has also done literacy a disservice. They point out that students no longer feel the need to learn the multiplication tables or to master correct grammar or spelling because the computer's software will provide the right answers. Although the computer is capable of many worthwhile functions, it does not teach an individual how to process words or develop an idea. Albert Shanker, president of the American Federation of Teachers, comments that "Life requires critical thinking skills, the ability to express yourself, persuade, argue, and build." Therefore, the computer is only as competent as its user, who may lack the basic skills of reading or writing.

Another electronic device blamed for the decline in literacy is the teaching machine. The teaching machine is a small box containing a tape upon which problems or questions have been programmed. The tape is organized so that the user proceeds from the simple to the complex. As the student answers the questions, he or she moves the tape ahead to find the correct answer. With little or no input from the teacher, students often find machine learning monotonous and their concentration limited. Further, questions that strike them concerning the taped lesson are often forgotten before they have an opportunity to ask the teacher about them. Bored and perhaps even disgusted with automatic teaching, the young people soon tune out.

Still another much-criticized device is the hand calculator. Small and easily carried about so that it can be used anywhere, it is blamed principally for a specific kind of illiteracy—mathematical illiteracy. As does the computer, it performs anything from simple to very complex mathematical tasks for us. We no longer need to do our own adding, subtracting, multiplying, and dividing. All we need to know is how to push the right keys.

Once again, we must compare the mind to a muscle. The electronic devices, from television to the hand calculator, reduce the amount of thinking we must do for ourselves. Without being challenged to think and reach decisions, the mind behaves exactly as does the muscle that is deprived of exercise. It weakens. As a result, it finds the tasks of learning—among them the job of learning and mastering the skills needed for successful reading and writing—too demanding to handle.

# WHY ILLITERACY: SOCIAL PROBLEMS

The nation's school system and the electronic developments that have influenced reading habits and classroom work are not totally to blame for the decline in our literacy rate. They are joined, in the view of many Americans, by a number of social factors, factors that include the current massive influx of immigrants, the poverty found everywhere in the country, and the decline in recent years of the American desire to achieve excellence in one's work.

## IMMIGRATION

America has long been called the "melting pot" of the world. It has attracted, accepted, and blended into its daily life millions of people from nations everywhere. The presence of people from so many different backgrounds has made us, culturally, one of the most interesting and diverse of countries. But there is no argument that the extremely heavy influx of the foreign-born in the past three decades has added greatly to the total of the nation's illiterates.[1] The reason is obvious: vast numbers of the new arrivals cannot speak, read, or write the English language.

Complicating matters is the fact that many of today's arrivals differ greatly from the immigrants who came to America just before and at the turn of the century. Most of those newcomers were eager to learn English and become active, participating citizens. Today, there is a tendency among the immigrants to cling to their native languages and to resist learning English.

At present, half a million people immigrate to the United States annually, with about half their number being Asians and Hispanics who, since the 1970s, have been fleeing the wars, economic problems, and political upheavals in their homelands. As you'll recall from chapter 1, the federal government estimates that the number of the nation's illiterates increases by 2 million a year. Immigrants are said to account for one-third of that total.

While the new arrivals have enriched America with their unique cultures, many immigrants have encountered a wide variety of problems, due in great part to their unfamiliarity with English. They have faced difficulties in finding and keeping jobs because of an inability to communicate effectively with employers. And those who are unwilling to learn English have lived with the burden of being culturally illiterate. They stand outside the mainstream of the nation's life, unable to grasp fully its traditions, helpless to comprehend all that goes on about them, and, consequently, finding it difficult—and sometimes impossible—to adjust to the ways of their new country.

It is estimated that during the 1990s, more than 5 million children of immigrant families will attend public schools in the United States. At present, more than 150 languages are used by teachers in classrooms across the nation.

The myriad languages are putting tremendous pressures on both teachers and school systems. Teachers who can speak only English, and perhaps a few words and phrases of another language, are daily faced with the trial not only of presenting their lessons but also of trying to help the youngsters understand what they are saying. The schools are faced with the task and expense of establishing bilingual programs and finding teachers to conduct them. Bilingual programs feature classrooms in which the native language of the foreign-born student is spoken.

In recent years, bilingual education has become the subject of a heated national debate. Those educators and members of the public who support it believe that it helps in learning English; once sufficiently comfortable in the new language, a student can then move on to a regular classroom. Opponents retort that this is a nice gesture on the part of the schools, but little more than a gesture. To substantiate their argument, they point to the New York City elementary school where 40 percent of the children are foreign born and from families that speak any one of twenty-six languages. They argue that the schools cannot find qualified teachers for all these languages and that it is economically unrealistic to expect them to do so. There is no doubt that the price tag is high. David Dolson, who is in charge of the bilingual programs provided by the California school system, admits that they are expensive and can add as much as 20 percent to the cost of educating each student.

Other charges are leveled at the bilingual approach. In a 1991 issue of *McCall's* magazine, Linda Chavez, senior fellow at the Manhattan Institute for Policy Research, claims that bilingual education fails Hispanic children. She writes that half the Hispanic junior high students in Boston's bilingual classes have been there for six years and are still unable to pass the tests given in basic English proficiency. Chavez believes that the non-English-speaking student should receive all instruction in English. Only as a last resort should the teacher answer any questions in the child's native tongue. In her opinion, total immersion in English is the fastest and best way to learn the language.

But there are those who disagree with this view. They hold that the total-immersion method bluntly tells the confused youngsters that they must "sink or swim" in America on their own, without any special treatment to help them.

But who is right and who is wrong? On the one hand, it does seem heartless to throw the newcomers, especially the youngest, into a room full of strangers speaking a strange language, and then expect them to fit in and learn without extra help. On the other hand, America *is* an English-speaking country. There is much evidence (for example, the black-Asian animosities that were seen during the 1992 riots in Los Angeles and elsewhere) to show that an inability to speak the national language does not meld the people into a unified whole but divides them into ethnic groups that are each isolated from and wary of the other. In the 1800s, this point was behind one of the guiding principles in the formation of the public school system. The principle, as explained in chapter 2, held that the system would be a success only if it taught a common language and a common appreciation of U.S. citizenship.

## POVERTY

Looming largest of the social problems that affect our country today and stand as barriers along the road to literacy is poverty.[2] Its most innocent victims are our children.

## The Children of Poverty

So much has been written about poverty that all of us, even if we have been raised in comfortable surroundings, can understand the evils that go hand in hand with it—the squalid housing, the ever-present specter of hunger, the feelings of hopelessness, the cruelties that those feelings too often trigger. To focus on how it erodes the spirits of children and contributes to lifelong illiteracy, we turn to the words of an elementary school teacher who works in a Los Angeles inner-city school:

*In my experience, I've found it not too difficult to interest very young children—the first- and second-graders—in reading. They're usually very curious about the words in their first books. The trouble usually starts when they grow a little older. Then so many of them simply stop wanting to learn. They hear their parents talk of how life holds out so little for the poor person. They hear their peers tell them they'll never get anywhere . . . that they'll be poor all their lives . . . that an education will do them no good . . . and that, if they're ever to have any money, they'd better get out there on the streets and steal it or go into drug dealing.*

*They believe what they hear—and considering what they see of their parents' lives and the adults around them, they've got plenty of reasons to believe it—and they turn against the whole idea of becoming educated. They don't see any value to it and so why try? They don't listen to what you're trying to teach them. They just sit there and stare at you or look out the window or start to act up and turn the room into a shambles. They refuse to participate in classroom work. You ask them a question and they tell you that they don't want to answer and won't. They stay away from school as often as they can.*

*The best that can be said is that, after learning a*

*little bit about reading and writing at the start of their schooling, they're going to remain functionally illiterate for the rest of their lives.*

*The rebelliousness and refusal to learn has a terrible effect on their teachers. The whole situation becomes a vicious circle. With the kids acting as they do, they [the teachers] finally give up on them and feel along with them that an education isn't going to do them a bit of good. And so they just pass them on from grade to grade. We call it baby-sitting. The kids finally leave school no better off than they were on their first day of school.*

The teacher goes on to say that drug abuse worsens the matter. While drug abuse today is a problem at all levels of our society, it is especially troublesome for kids in the inner city.

*Very early in life, the kids are pressured into the use of drugs by their peers and the drug dealers that haunt the neighborhood. Many want to become dealers themselves. They see the wads of money carried by the pushers. They see the big cars. The fancy clothes. The women. Those things all represent the "good life" and they want them for themselves. And they want them right now. So why bother trying to get an education? Why bother with learning to read, to write, or add a column of figures? None of these things will get them a thing in life. The only thing they'll need to know is how to add up the money they get from their customers. I've seen pushers as young as eight and nine years old. It's a tragedy.*

A twenty-year-old man named Joseph adds to the truth of what the teacher says when he speaks of his own experience with the pressures exerted by his peers on the streets. He grew up in a tough section of Brooklyn and he recalls that he felt isolated from the advantages that life has to offer and cut off from the possibility of ever working in a place more stimulating and challenging than a fast-food chain restaurant. In school, he says, he learned about Christopher Columbus and Martin Luther King— but not how to earn a living. His friends on the street, however, flaunted wads of cash and drove around in big cars. He soon desperately wanted to be part of the group that seemed "to have it all." Joseph committed a robbery, was apprehended, and was sent to jail.

After he served his sentence, Joseph attended Brooklyn's Prospect Heights High School, where he entered an American Express–sponsored work/study program. On graduating, he began working full-time as a computer operator at Shearson Lehman, an investment firm. He plans to go to college. He still lives with his mother.

His friends still urge him to push drugs and make a lot of money but Joseph shakes his head and plans to stay on his present course. Some of his friends drive around in an $80,000 Mercedes, causing Joseph, who doesn't own a car, to wonder at times if he is making the right choice. Then he remembers that some of his friends are dead— from drugs or drug-related violence. He says, "It's hard. These days, it seems to me, if you don't have money, nobody knows you."

But he balances that thought with another one: "Once you get on the wrong track, it's like a speeding train with no brakes."

### The Children of the Homeless
Within the past few years, a new stain has appeared in the fabric of poverty—homelessness. Groups that work with the homeless estimate that close to 3 million Americans are now on the streets because of the lack of affordable housing for the poor, unemployment, drug abuse, mental illness, and domestic violence.

Families with children account for more than half the homeless population in many cities, among them New York; Detroit; Portland, Oregon; Norfolk, Virginia; and Trenton, New Jersey. In other cities, such as San Francisco; New Orleans; Phoenix, Arizona; Minneapolis and St. Paul, Minnesota; and Charleston, South Carolina, they make up one-fifth or less of the homeless population.

The harm that homelessness can do to a child's education and literacy is dramatically illustrated in the case of eight-year-old Rose Marie, who presently lives in San Francisco. Rose Marie's mother is divorced. After the father abandoned the family several years ago, the mother struggled to support herself and her child by working in a container factory in Los Angeles. Two years ago, the factory closed down and, out of work, the mother and daughter have traveled to Dallas, Las Vegas, Nevada, and back to California in the hope of finding a job. Though Rose Marie's mother has managed to find employment from time to time, the two have spent most of their life on the streets. But the mother says that they have been among the "lucky" homeless and have been able to sleep in shelters most of the time. But she recalls one terrible night in Dallas, when all the shelters there were closed. The two spent the night huddled in the doorway of a small store, hungry, and as she says, "scared to death."

Life has gotten off to a poor start for Rose Marie and has been made all the worse by the fact that the child has been deprived of the full benefits of an education. She has attended school from time to time, but as her mother explains, she dislikes school, feels lost because she knows no one in class, and is discouraged because the other students are "way ahead of her."

Rose Marie cannot read or write. Her mother says plaintively that she would like her daughter to be able to do both.

According to a 1988 survey by the U.S. Department of Education, Rose Marie is one of an estimated 220,000 homeless school-age children. Of their number, more than 65,000 do not attend school regularly.

## The Children of Migratory Workers
Suffering much the same problem as Rose Marie are the children of migrant workers. They move on the average of three times a year as their families follow the crops. This means that, with each move, they have to adjust to a new community, new teachers and classmates, and often new rules and requirements. Forced to change schools and sometimes miss class because they are needed in the fields to help support the family, many of the children are years behind in their education.

In 1960, Congress passed the Migrant Children Education Assistance Act. The act established summer school programs for the migrant children, many of whom are Mexican-Americans, and ensured that their school records would be forwarded to the next school they attended. Although the act has helped, migrant children are still behind in schools.

## REVERSE PROBLEMS

Our talk of the social ills plaguing the United States and contributing to the rise of illiteracy has centered thus far on the harms done by poverty, drug abuse, and negative peer pressures. But what of the children who are not the products of poverty and who have been raised in comfortable and even affluent circumstances?[3]

They, too, are vulnerable to the dangers of drug abuse and negative peer pressures. Because they attend schools that are better equipped than those found in poor neighborhoods and because they stay in school longer than many poverty-stricken children, they are not threatened with becoming adults who are total illiterates. The danger is that they will emerge as functionally illiterate adults.

Just what are the other dangers they face? Take a very commonplace one that concerns real or imagined peer pressure—the ownership of a car. Most high school students would give anything to have a car, with many feeling that, without one, they will have trouble getting dates and winning friends. They see the car as a status symbol that attracts their peers to them. As a consequence, about two-thirds of all U.S. high school students work, not to help support their families but often to buy a car and then keep it running. To do so, many work twenty or more hours a week.

The problem may not seem a big one to most students. But Dr. Laurence Steinberg, a professor of psychiatry at Temple University, and Dr. Sanford Dornbusch, a professor of human biology at Stanford University, say that the opposite is true. They have researched the effects of part-time employment on 4,000 young people ranging in age from fifteen to eighteen and have found a strong link between working ten to fifteen hours a week and poorer grades, truancy, cheating, and the greater use of drugs and alcohol—all of which can contribute to an individual's illiteracy.

For many years, the children of affluent families shared a problem in their own way with the children of migratory workers. From the end of World War II until recently, many U.S. companies routinely transferred their top and middle management executives to plants and offices in various parts of the country. On average, the transfers uprooted the executives and their families and sent them to new locales every three years. The moves disrupted the continuity of the children's education and exerted a negative effect on their training in reading, writing, and other classroom subjects. Today, fortunately, most companies have reduced the number of transfers required of their executives.

A social problem that looms as a particular danger for the young person of an affluent family is the decline that has been noted in the desire of Americans for excellence of achievement. According to the National Commission on Excellence, which was commissioned by President Ronald Reagan in the early 1980s, the decline can be seen throughout the country. The commissioners define excellence as "performing on the boundary of individual ability in ways that test and push back personal limits, in school and in the workplace."

The commissioners are joined by countless Americans in saying that the past several decades have seen a malaise of mediocrity infect the United States. Instead of doing our best in any endeavor, they claim, we do no more than the required minimum. They argue that the malaise has been seen in the shoddiness of some American products and has been reflected in the kidding-for-real advice never to buy an American car that was made on a Monday morning or a Friday afternoon. They then point to the public school system and charge that the malaise is on view in the undemanding courses that high school students can take to earn credit toward graduation: preparation for adulthood and marriage, work experience outside the classroom, basket weaving, and physical education. The National Commission on Excellence, which edited *A Nation at Risk,* points out that 25 percent of all credits earned by high school students are for such courses, none of which teaches the literacy skills needed today for successful living but simply let the student "get by" on his or her way to graduation.

Jennifer serves as an example of "getting by" and then suffering for it later. She is from a well-to-do family and has recently graduated from high school. But her mother complains that, though Jennifer is able to read and write, she can do neither well enough to fill out a job application. Jennifer received credits toward her high school diploma in cheerleading, chorus, and basket weaving. Not one of these courses prepared her for the workplace. Not one of them improved her literacy skills.

Why has there been a decline in the desire for excellence of performance? Thoughtful Americans have come up with many possible reasons. Some claim that too many employees have grown far more interested in their salaries and their comfort at work than in their responsibility to do a good job. Others contend that the emphasis progressive education and many families have put on raising "happy" rather than ambitious children has ended up giving us unwilling workers when those children reach adulthood. Still others point to the boredom in much of the work done on factory production lines; they add that each production-line worker plays such a small role in the making of a product that he or she loses a sense of personal importance in its creation and feels little pride in the end product. Still others find a connection between the decline in excellence and the loss of faith in American ideals that so many people experienced during the Vietnam War.

Whatever the reason or combination of reasons for the decline, experts in literacy matters argue that it is essential for the nation, its schools, and its people to change their attitude toward the matter of excellence. They insist that we must demand a greater excellence of ourselves in all matters of living and put aside the idea that "just getting by" is good enough. If we fail to do so, we will continue to suffer increasing illiteracy and the problems that a nation must suffer when its people are unable to function successfully in their working, social, and intellectual lives; unable to participate in their community and national affairs; and no longer able to measure up to the standards set by the other leading nations of the world.

The growth of illiteracy in the United States is both dangerous and tragic. But as widespread as it now is, the situation is not hopeless. With determined effort, it can be ended. And, at present, a number of very determined efforts are already being made to end it.

# FIGHTING ILLITERACY: THE UNITED STATES

The battle against illiteracy is being fought at all levels of American society. Our federal, state, and local governments are participating. So are our school systems. And our business firms, from the largest to the smallest. And, of utmost importance, private citizens from every walk of life are joining the fight.

## THE FEDERAL GOVERNMENT

An important federal attack against illiteracy and other educational problems was launched in 1965. In that year, the U.S. Congress enacted the Elementary and Secondary Education Act (ESEA). The act, which was a part of President Lyndon B. Johnson's "War on Poverty," set into motion the nation's first major program of direct financial assistance to elementary and secondary schools. It initially provided funds for libraries, textbooks, research facilities, and experimental programs in various subjects and teaching techniques. A large share of the funds was directed to the schooling of the nation's poor families. The act, which has directed billions of dollars into education, has been revised and strengthened through the years and is responsible for many programs that remain in effect to this day.

A later attack came in September 1989, when President George Bush and the state governors met for a conference on the Charlottesville campus of the University of Virginia.[1] The subject of their discussion was the future of what they saw to be a dangerously faltering U.S. educational system. They all agreed that its improvement should be a matter of top national priority and established six major educational goals that are to be reached by the turn of the century. Listed under the general title "America 2000," the goals are:

*All children will be fit and healthy enough to start school and learn.*

*Ninety percent of the nation's students will graduate from high school. (At present, the high school graduation rate stands at about 70 percent.)*

*Students at all levels of learning must be competent in such basic subjects as English, mathematics, and science.*

*Every school will be free of violence and drugs.*

*Every American adult will be literate.*

*American high school students will rank first in the world in mathematics and science.*

In early 1991, Mr. Bush, who had long said that he wished to be known as the "Education President," announced a program meant to help the country achieve the six goals. His program contained several elements.

First, he advised that a set of national examinations be developed to keep track of how well students in the fourth, sixth, and twelfth grades are doing in the basic subjects of English, math, and science. Schools across the nation would not be forced to give the examinations but would be encouraged to administer them voluntarily. He hoped the tests could be developed and put to use by 1993.

Next, the president called on all American parents and business firms to become more involved in educational matters. He urged parents to take a deeper interest in their children's schoolwork and asked business firms to contribute up to $230 million to aid educational research.

Then, stressing that he hoped to "reinvent" the U.S. educational system and turn America into "a nation of students," Mr. Bush requested that Congress provide $620 million to finance upwards of 500 experimental schools whose job it would be to research and develop new methods of teaching.

The public reaction to the Bush plan was mixed. On the one hand, many Americans applauded it and said that it was sorely needed. Many, however, recognized that the illiteracy problem is overwhelming and that the year 2000 is close at hand. They felt that the six goals would probably not be achieved by that time. But they argued that the plan was moving the nation in the right direction and that the problem could eventually be licked.

On the other hand, there were widespread objections to certain provisions in the plan. Among the provisions most criticized was Mr. Bush's desire to see developed a national system of testing to measure student achievement. The complaint held that the testing, because it would measure performance against ambitious national standards set by the six goals, would not take into consideration the regional or cultural differences in the various school districts. Nor would it take into consideration the aims of the various districts. Many of the critics pointed out that minority students often fail in the standardized testing that already exists because it is too often designed for white, middle-class youngsters.

Regardless of such objections, Congress in August 1991 responded to the Bush plan by approving a bill that assigned $1.1 billion to "America 2000." The money was to be spent over a four-year period to fund a number of special programs. Funds were approved to meet the president's request for the establishment of the experimental schools and the development of the national testing system. The bill also set aside specific accounts for the following endeavors:

> *$60 million for family illiteracy programs. (These programs are meant for those families in which illiteracy is to be found among several or all members. Illiteracy has been present in many such families for generations.)*

> *$25 million for state literacy grants. (The grants are to help finance such efforts as programs for educating the illiterate and research into the circumstances causing a high rate of illiteracy within a state.)*

> *$2.5 million for local volunteer literacy programs. (As their name suggests, these programs are to be manned by community members who volunteer to teach reading to their less fortunate neighbors. Many such programs have been on the local scene for a number of years. We'll talk more about them in a later chapter.*

Further, the congressional bill allocated moneys to provide books for poor children with special educational needs, to help finance literacy programming on the nation's public broadcasting system (many of whose programs are telecast in the schools), and to fund special programs established by small businesses to eliminate illiteracy among their employees.

One aspect of Mr. Bush's plan did not make it into the congressional bill and has been the subject of a heated national debate ever since he proposed it. It is the proposal now widely known as "Choice." It gives parents the opportunity to choose where their children will attend school. They can opt for a public, private, or parochial school. For families earning less than $40,000 a year, "Choice" would provide vouchers amounting to $1,000 that they could spend at private or parochial schools. The voucher money would be paid by the states and come from their annual education budgets. The federal government would help to finance the program.

Mr. Bush called the proposal the "GI Bill for Children," likening the vouchers to the funds that were first given to veterans of World War II to spend where they wished for educational purposes. He said that the voucher system would accomplish two purposes. It would give middle- and low-income students the same chance as those of wealthier families to enter private or parochial institutions. And it would force the public schools to improve because of the competition posed by the private and parochial operations. The president contended that this competitive atmosphere would likewise stimulate the improvement of the private and parochial schools.

Opponents of the voucher approach argue that it would take tax money away from already tight state education budgets and place a heavy strain on school districts everywhere, because the districts receive public money on the basis of the average number of students attending class daily. In addition, the $1,000 voucher would be of no use to many families since it would not completely cover the tuition in most private and parochial schools. Others object to the voucher system because they believe it to be unconstitutional. They hold that it infringes on the First Amendment to the Constitution. Their feeling is that, with some of the voucher money going to parochial schools, the system violates America's separation of church and state.

If ever the voucher system is put into effect, Congress will have to approve $500 million to get it started.

## THE STATES AND THEIR
## LOCAL SCHOOL DISTRICTS

The federally appointed National Commission on Excellence warned in 1983 that "a rising tide of mediocrity" was spreading through the country's schools. The warning was voiced in the commission's final report, *A Nation at Risk*. Ever since, a number of states and their school districts have taken steps to stem the "rising tide" and, in the process, to reduce the illiteracy rate found in their midst.[2] We'll look first at the state actions. Here are two representative examples of what has been—and is being—done.

### Action at the State Level
Almost immediately in the wake of the commission's final report, South Carolina passed the Education Improvement Act of 1984, which called for compulsory kindergarten for five-year-olds and exit examinations for high school graduating seniors. The results brought by the act are impressive: the average scores posted on Scholastic Aptitude Tests (SAT), which are taken by all students hoping to enter college, have gone up 48 points since 1982, from 790 to 838 points; the number of students enrolled in advanced-placement courses has tripled since the 1983–84 school year; and absenteeism has dropped to 7.7 percent, which places South Carolina sixth in the United States in attendance.

State Superintendent of Education Charlie Williams believes that the change for the better has come about because educators, business leaders, political leaders, and parents have all worked together to improve the state's educational system. Further, to encourage a continuing improvement, the State Department of Education each year publishes a booklet titled *What Is the Penny Buying for South Carolina?* It reports on the latest advances being made, such as the rise in SAT scores, and singles out problems that still need attention, among them teacher salaries and the education cost per student.

In 1984, Governor Bill Clinton of Arkansas successfully promoted the passage of legislation that lengthened the school year in his state from 175 to 178 days. The legislation also called for a competency examination to be taken by the state's teachers. Participation in the test was voluntary, but teachers who refused to sit for it were faced with not having their teaching credentials renewed. Those who failed the examinations were not to be rehired. However, there was no restriction on the number of times the test could be taken and so some teachers tried as many as nine times before passing. Remedial workshops were held for the teachers who failed and who planned to retake the test. Out of the 37,326 teachers who first sat for the test, 1,354 (3.6 percent) failed.

The extended Arkansas school year was the future president's answer to a problem that has long troubled countless Americans: the fact that the nation has one of the shortest school years in the industrialized world and may be suffering because of it. In the United States, students attend class 180 days a year, as opposed to their West German and Japanese counterparts, who attend 210 and 243 days respectively. Many critics blame the shorter school year for the poor showing made by students when their academic performances are compared to those of their peers in other nations.

Many educators believe that one way to enhance the nation's educational system and make its graduates more effective when they enter the work force is to increase the number of school days. In the nineteenth century, young people needed the summer off to help their families on ranches and farms so it was expedient to have nine months of school and three months to help out on the family farm or ranch. Charles Ballinger, executive director of the National Association for Year-Round Education, says, "As far as I can see, there are very few students in Cleveland, Boston, New York, Miami, and San Francisco who need the summer off to work on the farm."

The idea of nine months of education and three months of vacation may soon become a thing of the past. School systems across the nation are looking with increasing interest at doing more than adding just a few days to the school calendar, as Governor Clinton did. They're looking at the idea of a year-round school with no summer vacation but shorter, intermittent holidays throughout the year.

Advocates of year-round education point to studies showing that students suffer from less learning loss with shorter holiday breaks. Ballinger calls the traditional three months of vacation "the long summer of forgetting." Studies also note better performance and fewer failing students and dropouts with the continuity of year-round schooling. Teachers in year-round classes report less burnout.

Opponents to the year-round approach are concerned that it will adversely affect family life by jeopardizing summer vacations and other family activities. For example, family outings could be complicated should brothers and sisters attend different schools with different holidays. There is also the problem of child care. With holidays spaced throughout the year, parents might find it more difficult than it is at present to arrange for child care.

## Action at the Local District Level

When we turn to what the nation's local school districts are doing to improve their offerings and to combat illiteracy, we find many already experimenting with the extended school year as a way to better their educational offerings and, in the process, reduce their illiteracy.

James Bradford, the superintendent of Buena Vista City Schools in Buena Vista, Virginia, has been operating an extended year at Parry McCluer High School since 1973. He believes that it actually costs more *not* to have a longer school year since such expenditures as salaries for the administrative staff and maintenance workers are on a yearly basis, as are textbooks, teacher benefits, and insurance costs. Granted, there are additional expenses for teacher salaries, utility fees, and bus operation, but these expenses, he states, are more than offset by the fact that fewer students have to repeat a grade. Also, juvenile delinquency caused by the summer complaint of nothing to do is much reduced. Bradford points out that the dropout rate in Parry McCluer High School has decreased, test scores have improved, and more McCluer students are attending college.

For the past three years, the Moton and Lockett schools just outside New Orleans have experimented with the extended school year. Juanita Smith, a second-grade teacher at Lockett, favors the extended year because the extra-long year gives the children a head start on the several weeks of review that are customarily needed at the beginning of each new term. She says, "Come September, I'm ready to get into the meat of reading. Normally in the traditional school year I can't do that until the end of October." Many parents approve of the extended year and believe their children are getting more out of school.

A different approach to the literacy problem was tried recently at the local district level, for three months in

Bellflower, a town in the Los Angeles area. Making it possible was Bellflower's Kaiser Permanente hospital and fifty-five volunteers who worked as tutors.

The hospital provided $15,000 for a "reading for hire" project. A portion of the money went to the purchase of books for the program. Then youngsters with the poorest reading habits and lowest literacy skills were "hired" to read the books with the help of the volunteers and were paid the remaining hospital money as a "salary" for doing so. The amount of their pay depended on the number of books they read.

At the close of the project, twelve-year-old Jarrod Manning had earned the largest salary. He began by reading at the first-grade level and finished at the sixth-grade level. Along the way, he had read sixty-four books, netting him a "salary" paycheck of ninety-six dollars.

Although financial gain certainly provided the original motivation for most of the children, Jeanie Cash, the principal at Woodruff Elementary School said that the youngsters soon proved they were more interested in reading the books than in earning the salaries. She said that they never came into her office and asked, "Where's my money?" Instead they'd ask when the volunteer tutor was coming.

Although the Bellflower teachers were at first skeptical of the reading-for-pay program, they saw not only an improvement in the children's reading ability but a decided improvement in their self-esteem as well.

## AMERICAN BUSINESS

Nancy J. Perry points out in a 1988 issue of *Fortune* magazine that although the taxes paid by corporate America make it a major contributor to public education, businesses are getting a poor return on their investment. She reports that each year 1 million teenagers drop out before graduating from high school. Most of them are unemployable. Those who do graduate often lack the problem-solving skills necessary to hold down a job in an increasingly complex workplace.

Recognizing the problem that it faces with an illiterate work force, corporate America has taken action in recent years.[3] For instance, Harold W. McGraw, Jr., retired chairman of McGraw-Hill Publishing Company, has organized the Business Council for Effective Literacy, whose purpose is to inform various corporations of the problem and seek their help in solving it. Many business leaders have answered his call. With a growing concern over the future work force's illiteracy, they have become involved in trying to help the educational system.

Today, Citicorp Bank offers in-service literacy help for some of its employees. American Express started the Academy of Finance, which is geared for the junior and senior high school student interested in banking, accounting, financial services, and business English. During the summer between their junior and senior years, the students participate in a paid internship.

At the Manhattan Center for Science and Mathematics, a new public school in New York's Spanish Harlem, General Electric spends $50,000 a year to help top students get into prestigious universities. It provides mentors and special classes for the young people who are known as GE Scholars. The Center is located on the site of the old Benjamin Franklin High School, which closed in 1982 after only 30 students in a class of 1,000 were graduated. In two years, 95 percent of the Center seniors have received diplomas. Today, with the help of General Electric, many minority students are preparing for careers in engineering and science.

Industries have developed technologies to help children and young people learn. A software program sold by International Business Machines (IBM) and called

"Writing to Read" has been very successful in teaching literacy skills to kindergarteners and first-graders in Pekin, Illinois. The program is easy for a youngster to use. First, it asks the child to write the word the way it sounds, for example, *enuf* for *enough* or *towl* for *towel*. Later, the child reads books that pair the words with their correct spellings. The Pekin superintendent of schools reports that the program has, in just two years, lowered the percentage of first-graders needing remedial help from 11 percent to 2 percent.

In Philadelphia, executives from forty companies including Continental Bank, Philadelphia Electric, and Rohm and Haas (a manufacturer of agricultural chemicals and plastics), have been involved for over twenty years in the Philadelphia High School Academies. This program for students from low-income families, devised by teachers and businesses, melds academic and vocational education with on-the-job experience. Business leaders consult with the teachers on a regular basis and help plan courses that meet the requirements of future employers.

United States business leaders are also keeping a concerned eye on the effectiveness of government-funded programs. One that both impresses and worries them is the Head Start preschool program. They are impressed by the fact that it has touched millions of children and that for every dollar it spends on a child, it saves the country six dollars later on in the costs of remedial education, welfare, and crime. But the business leaders are worried because, due to a tight federal budget, Head Start is able to accept less than 20 percent of children poor enough to qualify for it. David Kearns, the chairman of Xerox Corporation, remarks angrily, "It is one program we know is effective, and we still don't fully fund it. This is an outrageous misallocation of funds." President Bill Clinton has said that he favors full funding for Head Start.

Gone are the days when corporations did their civic duty by giving tickets to major-league baseball games as rewards to students with good attendance. Today, they are more likely to contribute to literacy programs or donate equipment, such as computers, directly to schools in their area. With predictions that the majority of new jobs in the next fifteen years will demand more than a mediocre high school education, American business is striving to build the future labor market.

# FIGHTING ILLITERACY: THE WORLD

Illiteracy is a global concern. It knows no borders. It is found among the people of all nations. As you'll recall from chapter 1, estimates hold that there are some 965 million adult illiterates in the world, with 98 percent of their number living in developing and Third World countries. Because they are illiterate, these 965 million adults are denied access to the knowledge and information that could enable them to participate in and contribute to the political, economic, and cultural activities in their countries. And because they are unable to participate and contribute, they have long been known as the forgotten people of the world.

But due to work now being done at the international level and in a growing number of individual countries, the hope is high that global illiteracy can be reduced and that increasing numbers of these people will no longer be the world's forgotten ones.

## AT THE INTERNATIONAL LEVEL

A major branch of the United Nations—The United Nations Educational, Scientific, and Cultural Organization (UNESCO)—is leading the fight against illiteracy at the international level.[1] The organization has been active in promoting literacy since 1946, a year after the United Nations itself was formed. Today, UNESCO provides training services worldwide and serves as an adviser to countries struggling to overcome the illiteracy within their borders.

At present, the organization is embarked on a program called Plan of Action 1990–1999. The Plan hopes to achieve the same ambitious goal worldwide that America 2000 is seeking for the United States: a major reduction in the illiteracy rate, if not its total eradication, by the turn of the century.

In 1990, UNESCO got the Plan started with what it called the International Literacy Year (ILY). The purpose of the Year, which was formally launched on December 6, 1989, was to initiate activity worldwide for the spread of literacy. To do this, UNESCO in 1990:

*Called for governments to take action to end total and functional illiteracy wherever it was found within their borders—in rural areas, in city slums, among women and girls and people with special educational needs.*

*Sought to make the people of all countries aware of the magnitude of global illiteracy and solicited their help in finding ways to overcome it. The organization spread the word by issuing news releases, publishing informational materials, and sponsoring literacy conferences.*

*Urged the member nations of the UN to help each other—and all other countries—in the struggle against illiteracy.*

The ILY triggered two major conferences. The first was actually held in 1989, when media representatives from all over the world met at UNESCO's Paris headquarters to discuss what they could do to help promote the Year. As a result of the meeting a major Japanese newspaper launched a campaign to collect a yen ($1.00 equals approximately 127 yen) for each illiterate in Asia and the Pacific. (There are about 700 million illiterates in the region.)

Then, in early 1990, UNESCO sponsored an international literacy conference at Jomtien, Thailand. Joining in the sponsorship were the World Bank, the United Nations Development Programme (UNDP), and the United Nations Children's Fund (UNICEF). Some 1,500 representatives from governments, private agencies, and educational organizations attended and pledged themselves to meet the following goals by the year 2000: a halving of the 1990 global illiteracy rate, a common level of learning achievement for 80 percent of all fourteen-year-old boys and girls, and an equaling of the literacy rates for males and females. As was said in chapter 1 and will be stressed later in this chapter, the illiteracy rate for women has always been substantially higher than that for men.

Helping to further the work of the Plan of Action are UNESCO programs that have long been in effect. For example, each September 8, which is observed as International Literacy Day, the organization awards several prizes to groups that have promoted literacy in various countries. In 1989, Nigeria, Mauritania, Jamaica, and Indonesia received awards for their literacy programs, all of which tied the teaching of reading to stories and ideas of local culture. This made the instruction all the more interesting and meaningful for the students.

UNESCO has long sponsored projects that work in various ways to eradicate illiteracy. One is the UNESCO Co-Action Program, which operates in small communities. In such countries as Kenya, Mali, Nepal, and Peru, the program has refurbished local schools. In Lebanon and Africa's Sierra Leone and Burkina Faso (formerly Upper Volta), it has provided the learning centers there with reading materials, paper, pencils, and other needed equipment. It has purchased Braille equipment for the blind in more than twenty-six nations.

Another UNESCO project, the Special Account for World Literacy, recently sponsored a training program for semi-literate women in China. The program not only worked to improve the women's reading and writing skills but also helped them to master basic mathematics. UNESCO reports that, as a result, the women saw an improvement in their job skills, which, in turn, raised their self-esteem and promised to increase their pay at work.

## AT THE NATIONAL LEVEL

On their own—and often with UNESCO assistance—a growing number of nations are attacking the illiteracy within their borders.[2] Their aims and achievements have been notable:

*Ever since 1949, the People's Republic of China has waged a campaign to end its widespread illiteracy problems. The campaign has been principally aimed at rural areas, where 91 percent of the nation's approximately 230 million illiterates live. It has improved classroom instruction there and has established seventeen technical schools where farmers are not only taught to read and write but to develop their agricultural skills. In the more than forty years since its inception, the campaign has seen upwards of 150 million people learn to read and write and has reduced China's illiteracy rate from 80 percent to 34.5 percent. During the International Literacy Year, the Chinese government announced a new campaign, this one meant to reduce the literacy rate by yet another 10 percent.*

*As the 1990s dawned, the government of India announced that it planned to spend $2 billion to help 80 million illiterates between the ages of fifteen and thirty-five learn to read and write. This goal is to be reached by 1995.*

*In Africa, Ethiopia launched a literacy program in 1979 with the aim of reaching 1.3 million people in its urban and rural areas. More than 10 million people participated in the effort, with 4 million of their number becoming literate by 1983. In that year, Ethiopia reported that its illiteracy rate was down from 93 percent to 44.8 percent. In recent years, Ethiopia's literacy efforts have suffered because of the drought and civil strife that have plagued the nation.*

*And in another part of the world, Canada in 1988 inaugurated an extensive literacy program. The nation is investing $110 million (Canadian dollars) in the endeavor over a period of five years.*

One of the greatest success stories in the global battle against illiteracy comes from Cuba and dates as far back as 1960.

Located approximately ninety miles off the southern U.S. coast, Cuba is an island country about the size of Pennsylvania. Once a Spanish holding, it gained its independence in 1902 and then, more than five decades later, became a communist nation when Fidel Castro led a successful revolution against the government in 1959.

One of the first tasks that Castro undertook after establishing himself as prime minister was the eradication of Cuban illiteracy. His principal targets were the nation's rural areas, where the illiteracy rate was running at 41.7 percent and where schools were a rarity.

Prior to Castro, Cuba's educational problems had been many. The average number of years that children from poor families spent in school were four—if the youngsters went to school at all.

Although public education (when it was available) was free, the classrooms were vastly overcrowded. Teachers were often incompetent and frequently absent. There were only twenty-one secondary schools in the country. The clergy operated some private schools, but they were expensive and generally poor in quality. University education was limited to the wealthy and was concentrated on producing lawyers and journalists. Colleges neglected to include courses for desperately needed engineers, agronomists, teachers, and technicians of all types.

Aside from recognizing the need for an educated populace if his country was to survive and develop, Castro had two other reasons for placing such emphasis on literacy. First, literacy would foster economic and cultural advancement in a country suffering from underdevelopment. At the time, Cuba was completely dependent upon agriculture, but the country was rich in mineral resources that were waiting to be tapped, a job that could be successfully done only by literate citizenry. Second, by teaching the people to read and write, he could indoctrinate them in the ideas and policies of his revolutionary movement.

The prime minister displayed his flare for the dramatic when he went before the General Assembly of the United Nations in September 1960. He grandly announced that his country was starting a new life by preparing for the "Year of Education." The year, 1961, was to be dedicated to an intensive literacy campaign.

He appointed a National Literacy Commission to be in charge of preparing for the campaign. Under the commission's direction, 1.5 million copies of an illustrated primer, made up of fifteen lessons and entitled *Ven-*

*ceremos* ("We Shall Overcome"), were printed. A teaching manual for the instructors entitled *Alfabetizadores* ("To Make Literate") was also published.

The campaign called for the major work to be handled by voluntary, unpaid instructors under the training and supervision of professional teachers. More than 120,632 volunteers were eventually involved in the Year's labor. Joining them were 34,772 professional teachers.

During the first quarter of 1961, the commission worked out the final details of the campaign and launched a massive publicity drive on its behalf. The drive utilized all available media: newspapers, radio, television, and public meetings. Even hymns and songs were composed and circulated. The extensive publicity served two purposes. It helped recruit instructors and triggered a great enthusiasm among the illiterate population. Daily heard was the slogan: "If you can teach, teach; if you can't teach, learn."

The second quarter of the year saw the enlistment of twelve- to eighteen-year-old *brigadistas* ("young students") for the volunteer force. They were excused from their schoolwork and were sent into Cuba's primitive countryside, with some venturing into the rugged and remote Sierra Maestra mountain range and the swampy Zapata Peninsula. For their coming work, they were outfitted with uniforms, hammocks, blankets, and two simple manuals: one for the learner and one for the tutor.

It was a unique experience for the young urban volunteers. Many of them had never been out of their cities or towns. Many were from the comfortable homes of the well-to-do. Most had never come into contact with peasants and the hard ways of rural life.

In addition to adjusting to new surroundings, the volunteers had to adjust to their pupils' work schedules. Often, the only time the peasants weren't working in the fields was at night. Then, with only a flashlight or kerosene lanterns at hand, a young tutor and the family of illiterates would gather around a table and explore the wonders of the written word.

When a district's population had learned the basics of reading and writing, a flag was flown, signifying the success of that particular area. Soon the various regions were competing with each other to be the first to fly the flag of literacy.

As planned, the massive effort ended with the close of 1961. But it achieved remarkable results. It sent Cuba's illiteracy rate plunging to 3.9 percent, which put it almost on a par with America's 3.2 percent rate in 1950. More than 707,000 adults had learned to read and write.

Of course, in the time that was allotted to the campaign, the learner could only be brought to an elementary stage of literacy. But Cuba has followed up its Year of Education with a broad adult education program, plus a system of "home reading circles" where individuals who are unable to attend the adult education courses can meet with others to read under the guidance of amateur teachers.

In the years immediately following the campaign, Cuba began building new schools and teaching subjects of practical value to agriculture and industry.

Today, the nation's young people are required to attend school until they are at least fourteen years old. The budget for education is double what it was in the pre-Castro years.

A UNESCO commission visited Cuba in 1963, and pointed out several factors that favored the literacy campaign. First, the nation's illiterate population was at a manageable size in comparison to those of Asiatic countries, where illiteracy was far more widespread. Second, the government was strong and powerful enough to see that its program was carried out. Third, since Spanish is the language of Cuba, there was no language barrier to hamper the instruction, as would be the case in a country in which various languages and dialects are spoken.

The commission, however, remarked that more than anything else, the success of Cuba's Year of Education was the result of human relationships—one human being helping another.

## THE WORLD: WOMEN AND ILLITERACY

In a remote village in India, ten-year-old Fatiah lives with her parents and four brothers. Her mother and father are agricultural workers and Fatiah sometimes helps in the field. Fatiah would like to go to school and learn to read and write, but the school is many miles from her home. To further complicate her plight, the teacher is a man and so because of their cultural beliefs, her parents will not allow her to attend.

Fatiah is just one of an estimated 100 million children of primary-school age who do not attend school and who, by the next century, will add to the number of adult illiterates worldwide.[3] To make matters worse, as a female, she is a member of the vast group that suffers the greatest degree of illiteracy. UNESCO reports the sad fact that, of the world's 965 million adult illiterates, fully 637 million—or two-thirds of the total—are women. The figure is even greater in some predominantly rural countries. There, more than 90 percent of the female population are helpless when faced with the written word.

There are numerous reasons for the deplorable state of illiteracy among women. In some societies, such as is the case with Fatiah, the reasons are cultural. In some, male domination is at fault. In such regions as Asia, Africa, and Latin America, female illiteracy is linked to poverty, the traditional division of social roles between the sexes, and systems of education that make it difficult for girls and young women to enter school.

Further, there are all the tasks that the woman has been called upon to do over the centuries—cooking, cleaning, fetching water and firewood, helping in the fields, and rearing her children. They have left her with little time or energy for learning to read and write. Still another factor plays a major role in her illiteracy: the attitudes of those men who feel threatened by the possibility that she will learn more than they and will challenge their position of authority in the home, the community, and the workplace.

Still another factor emerges: Research has shown that, when women and girls in Third World nations have learned to read and write, they are likely to allow their newly acquired literacy skills to dwindle because the reading material that would meet their needs and interests is not available and their time to read is limited because of their daily chores.

Fortunately, for a number of years, a global effort has been under way to reduce women's illiteracy and to eventually eradicate it. A major thrust of UNESCO's International Literacy Year was to promote a worldwide awareness of a woman's problems and to launch a number of teaching campaigns on her behalf. One such campaign was seen in Peru, where UNESCO sent a traveling instructional project throughout the nation's remote areas.

The ILY also saw the United Nations Development Programme (UNDP) in the midst of a Nepalese literacy project. Its purpose was to improve Nepal's rural development by teaching young out-of-school girls to read, write, and practice good health habits. Instruction was given by women to soothe the misgivings of families who disliked the idea of seeing their daughters attend schools where the sexes were mingled. As is the case in many of the literacy programs sponsored by individual nations, the instruction in reading and writing was joined with advice on good health habits. Research through the years indicates that poor health in children is strongly linked with female illiteracy.

The literacy programs conducted by individual nations are many. Senegal, Kenya, Burkina Faso, and Tanzania are just four of the African countries sponsoring such efforts. Burkina Faso's program was launched in 1988 with the goal of teaching 13,000 rural women to read and write. Attending were women from ten language groups. During the course of their instruction, they lived in what were called "boarding centers" that were provided by the nation's Ministry of Rural Affairs. The women were allowed weekly breaks to go home and visit their families.

Tanzania's effort, dating back to 1981, is one of the oldest in Africa. At that time, many Tanzanian men did not welcome the idea of the program, fearing that female literacy might undermine their authority. But the program was established with the help of the country's leading figures.

The fruit that the national literacy programs for women has borne can be clearly seen in two examples from widely separated regions. First, a woman in New Delhi, India, reports that she was functionally illiterate until age thirty-five, when she entered a year-long literacy course. Following the course, which also featured instruction in basic accounting, she was able to find a much-needed job. Further, she and a number of her classmates became active in pushing for clean water and improved sanitation and garbage collection in their neighborhood.

The second example comes from Africa's Kenya. There, a group of newly literate women, when answering a questionnaire distributed by the World Young Women's Christian Association (YWCA) in the late 1980s, spoke of how literacy had brought them a great sense of pride and self-reliance. One woman expressed delight at being able to read the instructions on a medicine bottle. Another said that literacy, which included a grasp of mathematics, gave her more control over money matters in her family. In their replies to the questionnaire, the women also expressed these views on the improved position in life won by the woman who has taken literacy training:

*She is more respected both in the community and home.*

*She is better able to find employment and to earn more.*

*She comes to know that she is capable of doing jobs that have been traditionally restricted to men.*

*She is able to operate a business of her own and keep records on her own.*

*She can be an effective leader of women's groups.*

*She gains a greater understanding of her rights.*

*She becomes better able to help in the education of her children.*

*Her political awareness is improved, as are the skills that enable her to participate in and organize groups and events.*

In the light of all opinions expressed by the newly literate Kenyan women, the significance of female literacy to the world cannot be overstated. Once literate, the woman becomes an active participant in and contributor to her society rather than a passive observer. Further, UNESCO director-general Frederico Mayor touches the heart of the matter when he calls women "the mothers of a literate society." As the mothers of all the coming generations, it is vital that women be literate if they are to lead those generations to literacy and the ability to contribute to the world's well-being.

The global battle being waged against illiteracy is a great one and is winning victories on many fronts. But it is also an uphill struggle. As great numbers of people leave the ranks of the illiterate each year, greater numbers enter those ranks. Further, especially in countries still in the early stages of their development, the battle is being slowed by such problems as inadequate educational systems, poor health care, homelessness in the large cities, poverty, and unemployment.

It is hoped, however, that the slow and steady growth of literacy will eventually help to solve these problems. The illiterate are helpless to solve public problems and rectify public wrongs. Only the literate have the ability to participate in or, better yet, instigate attacks on the myriad social ills in their midst.

S
E
V
E
N

# FIGHTING ILLITERACY: PROGRAMS AND VOLUNTEERS

There are four major national literacy programs in the United States. Two are federal projects:

**Adult Basic Education**

**The remedial training program for military recruits.**

The remaining two of the four programs are privately supported:

**Laubach Literacy Action**

**Literacy Volunteers of America.**

In addition to these four, there are many state and municipal programs. They are supported by business leaders, librarians, educators, and volunteer workers. But no matter whether a program is national, state, or local in nature, it shares a common goal with all the others: the successful teaching of reading and writing to an individual.

## ADULT BASIC EDUCATION

Adult Basic Education is the largest and oldest literacy program in the nation. It differs in two ways from the general adult education programs that are found in all the states. First, it is federally funded while general adult education in a state is funded by the state itself and/or the community. Second, the general adult education programs offer all types of courses of interest to the public. Adult Basic Education concentrates on literacy skills and, as its name suggests, provides the student with a basic education.

Ranging upward in age from sixteen, the students who enroll in Adult Basic Education classes are usually of three types. Some are immigrants eager to learn to read and write in English. Some, who may be either American or foreign born, want to improve on whatever beginning literacy skills they have already acquired so that they can get better jobs or play a greater role in community events. Some attend because their weakness in reading and writing was one of the factors that caused them to drop out of school before they received a high school diploma. They are now after the training that will enable them to take the required courses for a General Education Diploma.

For more than half the students, the program proves a success. It turns some 60 percent of their number into literate adults. Unfortunately, according to Jonathan Kozol in his book, *Illiterate America*, the remaining 40 percent fail to achieve their goal.[1] Some drop out because the classes are not conveniently scheduled. Others object to the distance they must travel to class. Still others, who did not like school as youngsters, say that they cannot tolerate the program because, as one has put it, "Adult Basic Education is just another name for school."

Germaine was one student who did not drop out. Dressed in bib overalls and wearing men's boots, she brought her nineteen-year-old son to an Adult Basic Education class in Novato, California. She said, "John wants to join the Navy. I told him that first he had to get his 'piece of paper' (General Education Diploma) so I brung [*sic*] him to class." Each week, Germaine arrived with a reluctant John in tow. The teacher asked her if she wouldn't like to take some courses along with John, but she shook her head. But, after her son had received his GED certificate and enlisted in the Navy, Germaine returned to class. She told the teacher, "I couldn't shame John by letting him know I couldn't read. I came from a large family and a lot of times I couldn't go to school because both my parents worked and someone had to take care of the young ones. But now, I'm here. And I'm going to learn to read and by the time John comes home, I'll know how." And she did![2]

## THE MILITARY'S REMEDIAL PROGRAM

During World War II, as you'll recall from chapter 2, the U.S. Army reported that it was forced to reject many young men because they were unable to understand the kinds of written instructions necessary for carrying out basic military tasks. Ever since, the services have complained of the discouraging number of young Americans who are unable to read instructions, comprehend test questions, and write simple communications.

To protect their equipment from harm by personnel unable to read instructional manuals and to make certain that all personnel can read and understand military orders, the armed forces have conducted literacy programs for totally and functionally illiterate recruits ever since World War II.

Joe was one such recruit. When he enlisted in the Army in 1944, he could barely read or write. Despite this, he proved to be a good soldier and, after he had been in uniform for a few months, his sergeant advised him to take the test for the rank of corporal. Joe shook his head and replied that he wasn't "very good in the reading department."

"We can fix that," the sergeant said, and, as Joe recalls, "The next thing I knew, I was in the camp literacy program." There, he learned to read and write well enough to pass the test for corporal. When he left the army at the war's end, Joe went to work for the utility company in his hometown and spent his evenings taking additional remedial classes at a nearby junior college. In time, Joe brought his reading ability up to eighth-grade level.[3]

Some educators have criticized the military literacy program because it does not seek to "round out" a recruit's education by instructing him in subjects such as history and literature. But the services reply that their program is strictly a military one and is aimed at turning recruits into literates solely for the purpose of understanding written military orders and written instructions for the safe handling and efficient maintenance of military equipment.

So Joe was not coached in history or Shakespeare, but he did learn to read and write and then later took steps on his own to hone his literacy skills and broaden his education. He plans to retire soon from his job, and his appreciation of the literacy training he received in the army can be heard whenever he says, "People always ask, 'What are you going to do when you retire?' I tell them I'm going to teach someone to read."[4]

## LAUBACH LITERACY ACTION

This literacy program was started by Dr. Frank C. Laubach (1882–1970), a Congregational missionary.[5] In 1915, after graduating from New York City's Columbia

University, Dr. Laubach traveled to the Philippines to do pastoral work among the Moro people of Mindanao. With the help of Donato Galia, a Filipino colleague, Laubach set about learning the Maranaw language and committing it to writing. By the time he finished what turned out to be an immense task, he had committed twenty-one local languages to writing. At the same time, he developed a system of teaching the people to read and write.

He began creating his system with the words in the languages he had committed to writing. He turned them into word lists from which primer reading books could be constructed. Then he established a three-step teaching program:

> 1. *Using the word lists, the students first learned to connect the letters in the words with their sounds and meaning.*

> 2. *Next, they learned to read between 200 and 400 words in the Laubach primers. The primers were written so that they contained words that would unfailingly catch the students' interest. For example, they always featured the names of local villages and the various islands in the Philippine chain. Another example: For the many pupils who were fishermen, the primers were filled with words pertaining to fishing.*

> 3. *Finally, once they had completed their work with the primers, the students were urged to continue using their reading and writing skills in their daily lives. In this way, they would become more and more proficient in these skills as time passed.*

Along with establishing the three-step program, Dr. Laubach developed two principles that his system of teaching was always to follow. He devised the two principles because he knew that he would have to depend on volunteer instructors (including the ones he had taught) if his program was to be carried out on all of the islands in the Philippines. The principles were to serve as guides for every volunteer. He gave them the following names:

Learnability: *The term meant that each lesson was to be short, swift, and of compelling interest to the students.*

Teachability: *The lessons had to be constructed so that anyone who learned them could then teach them to someone else. Some of the lessons had to be built so that the student could learn them without the help of an instructor.*

Dr. Laubach also stressed that, since the illiterate usually—if not always—suffers a sense of inferiority, instructors should never appear superior to a student. They should always teach with compliments rather than discouraging corrections and should never ask questions that they know a student cannot answer. Should a pupil ever hesitate in giving an answer, an instructor should avoid an embarrassing pause and give the information immediately.

Finally, Dr. Laubach told all the instructors that they should never attempt to teach pupils they did not like. He said that, although an illiterate cannot read the printed word, he or she can read human nature.

The program, to which the doctor gave the slogan "Each one teach one," proved such a great success that, when he returned to the United States in 1936, the Philippine government took over his system and used it in a broad anti-illiteracy campaign. What were called "Literacy Wagons," loaded with instructors and reading materials, traveled throughout the islands. Wherever they went, they gathered illiterate adults together for reading and writing classes. As a result of the campaign, the government announced that the nation's prisons were becoming universities and that the Filipino army was almost 100 percent literate by the time the war with Japan erupted in 1941.

Convinced that his methods could be applied to the illiteracy problems in other nations, Dr. Laubach visited Malaya, India, Egypt, Palestine, Syria, Turkey, and the African countries of Tanzania (formerly Tanganyika, Zanzibar, and Pemba) and Kenya. In each, he talked with missionaries and others who were interested in the cause of literacy, helped them to make word lists in thirty languages, and guided them in establishing his program. Ultimately, his program found its way to the entire world. For his work, Dr. Laubach long ago was christened "the father of literacy."

The Laubach program today operates worldwide under the name Laubach Literacy International. The American program, which was founded in 1955, is known as Laubach Literacy Action and is a branch of the international organization.

## LITERACY VOLUNTEERS OF AMERICA

Some thirty years ago, while reading her local newspaper, Ruth Colvin of Syracuse, New York, came upon an article about a recent survey by the U.S. Bureau of the Census. The article stated that the survey revealed that 11,055 illiterate adults lived in her city. She knew that illiteracy plagued many underdeveloped countries. But illiteracy in America? She was both shocked and dismayed—and then determined to help correct the problem.[6]

To begin, Ruth Colvin checked with the Syracuse schools and discovered that very little was being done to help those 11,000 plus; worse, no one seemed to know for certain who they were and how they could be helped. With this information in hand, she invited a number of community leaders to her home to discuss the situation and what steps could be taken to remedy it. From that grassroots beginning, Ruth Colvin went on to found the Literacy Volunteers of America (LVA).

She found it easy to secure volunteer instructors for the first classes presented by LVA. People from all walks of life in Syracuse wanted to lend a hand. But a difficulty soon appeared in the question of how to train the volunteers to do an effective job. For the answer, Ruth Colvin turned to Laubach Literacy Action and asked for teaching materials and instructions. Armed with the Laubach materials, she and her volunteers held their first classes. They recorded a number of successes and failures. Frustrated by the failures, she sought help from the reading clinic at Syracuse University.

It was a wise move on her part. The clinic provided her with several teaching techniques that, when combined with the Laubach materials and the growing experience of her volunteers, saw LVA record an increasing number of successes over the years.

One of the most interesting of the techniques advised by the reading clinic is called "language experience" or "experience stories." When using it, the volunteer instructor asks a nonthreatening question, such as "Do you have any hobbies?" The student might reply, "I like to sew." The instructor writes the exact words on the chalkboard, saying each word aloud as it is written. The instructor then asks the student to "read" what is written. Reading is simple because the student recalls what has been said, but at the same time, is impressed because his or her thoughts are important enough to write down and read. At work here is an idea much like Dr. Laubach's insistence that literacy teaching should always compliment rather than discourage the nonreader.

Over the past three decades, Literacy Volunteers of America has become a national organization. LVA presently has more than 80,000 participants in the United States and Canada.

## LOCAL PROGRAMS AND VOLUNTEERS

The four national programs are joined by state and local programs that are found in all parts of the nation.[7] The former are customarily presented under the banner of state departments of education. The local programs have a wide variety of sponsors: churches, community colleges, the YMCA and YWCA, libraries, civic and private organizations, and business firms.

A local program may be presented to small groups of students or to single individuals. It may use any of several different instructional approaches. It may follow the Laubach system, which is grounded in the phonics approach to teaching. It may employ the whole-word method, which is taught in many of today's public schools. (To refresh your memory on the phonics and whole-word methods, see chapter 3.) It may use a combination of the two. Or it may come up with a teaching system of its own devising.

Though their teaching methods may differ, all the local programs share two characteristics. First, they depend on volunteers as instructors. Second, they submit the volunteers to a training program and acquaint them with all the teaching materials before allowing them to work with a student.

Some programs provide instruction in English as a Second Language (ESL) for the foreign-born and their children. A knowledge of the student's language is not necessary for someone who wishes to volunteer to teach ESL. Again, training is given to the volunteer before he or she goes to work with a non-English-speaking pupil.

The teaching afforded by the local programs can be done in any of a number of settings. Some programs call for the student to come to a particular place, perhaps a school classroom, but usually the student and volunteer mutually agree on the time and location for getting together. They may decide to meet in a room in the local library or church, in one another's home, or in one another's workplace.

The volunteers come from all walks of life, as can be seen in the literacy program sponsored by the library in a small California city. Among those working in the program are several housewives, a widow, a retired banker, two retired air force officers, two retired teachers, and a college sophomore.

Of particular interest to young people who would like to volunteer is a program that has been spreading among high schools. Known as the "peer program," it calls for students to work on a one-to-one basis with fellow students who are having trouble developing their reading and writing skills. The program is realizing much beginning success because it often sees a friend of the troubled student serving as his or her instructor. The rapport between the two creates an easy atmosphere that facilitates the learning process.

For the volunteer in any program—from the national to the local level—the experience is, almost without exception, a highly rewarding one. There is the deep satisfaction that comes from helping another. A California volunteer says she will never forget how deeply touched she was when one of her students, a father, expressed the joy he felt on finally being able to read a story to his son. She recalls that, for the first time in her life, she felt she had made a positive difference in someone's life.

Even more important in the minds of many volunteers is the fact that they have learned valuable lessons from their students. One volunteer, speaking for many on this point, remarks that she had a student who came from poverty-stricken circumstances and suffered one humiliation after another because he was functionally illiterate. The determination he showed in learning to read and write so he could improve life for his family and himself impressed her deeply and convinced her that, "if you want something badly enough in life, you can get it." She adds that the strength he showed gave her a new confidence in her own talents.

Other volunteers say that tutoring in literacy programs has inspired them to pursue their own dreams. A middle-aged volunteer who has long wanted to open his own business says, "I know of a man who learned to read and write when he was in his nineties. If he could do that, then I can go after my own dream and I intend to do exactly *that*." The man to whom the volunteer refers ranks as one of the most unusual successes in the history of Laubach Literacy Action, David Eugene Ray of Franklin, Tennessee.

Mr. Ray, who lives in a retirement home, never attended school, but went to work as a hired hand when he was seven. He spent his life raising pigs and planting corn, beans, and potatoes. He figured all his financial transactions in his head.

When it was discovered at the nursing home that Mr. Ray couldn't read, one of the staff asked if he would like to learn. He nodded and said that he would give it a try. Once a week, a Laubach volunteer tutored him at the nursing home. Recently, David Eugene Ray celebrated his one hundredth birthday. For the first time in his life, he could read his birthday greeting cards.

In all, while learning to read and causing the volunteers to feel a deep sense of satisfaction, the students teach the volunteers at least three valuable lessons, doing so by their example. They teach courage, the courage to confront their illiteracy; determination, the determination to learn, no matter their age; and humility, the humility that enables them to admit their lack and seek help to overcome it.

Wally "Famous" Amos, who has won national renown for the manufacture of cookies, perhaps says it best of all. He is a spokesman for Literacy Volunteers of America and he describes volunteering as: "Reaching with your hand into the darkness to pull another person's hand back into the light, only to discover that the hand you hold is your own."

# JOINING THE BATTLE

Globally, illiteracy touches not only the 965 million people afflicted with it, but also the thousands of people who are fighting everywhere to end it. The ranks of these fighters must swell if the problem is to be eradicated within the foreseeable future. This means that we all must lend a hand, no matter whether we are young or old.

As a young person, you may be reluctant to join the ranks of those fighting illiteracy. You may think you are too young to help or that there is little of value that an individual can do. Actually, on both counts, the reverse is true. Your help is needed and there is much of value that you can do as a young person and an individual. Here are six ideas that, starting even today, you can put to use.

## 1. LEARN ABOUT THE PROBLEM

You've already taken the first step in this direction. Reading this book has served as an introduction to the problem. But there is still much, much more to learn. To help further broaden your knowledge and understanding of illiteracy and its dangers, here is a list of other books on the subject. They make interesting and valuable reading.

Read with Me. *Walter Anderson. Houghton Mifflin Company, 1990.*

Illiterate America. *Jonathan Kozol. New American Library, 1986.*

Prisoners of Silence. *Jonathan Kozol. Continuum Publishing Corporation, 1980.*

The above books are among the latest on the market and contain much up-to-date information. There are, however, three older books that can prove helpful, especially as histories of the illiteracy problem:

Tomorrow's Illiterates. *Charles C. Walcutt, Editor. Little, Brown and Company, 1961.*

Illiteracy: A World Problem. *Sir Charles Jeffries. Praeger Publishers, 1967.*

The New Illiterates. *Samuel L. Blumenfeld. Arlington House, 1973.*

These books and a number of others can usually be found at your local library. You'll also discover much information in magazines and your local newspaper. Still more information can be gathered by writing to organizations that are working on the illiteracy problem. One such organization is the Project on Adolescent Literacy, which has been collecting and reviewing research into illiteracy since 1985. You can obtain information and ask questions of the project by writing to its information office at the following address:

*Project on Adolescent Literacy*
*Center for Early Adolescence*
*University of North Carolina at Chapel Hill*
*Suite 211 Carr Mill Mall*
*Carrboro, North Carolina 27510*

If you wish further information on the actions being taken against illiteracy throughout the world, you can write to the United Nations Educational, Scientific, and Cultural Organization (UNESCO) at:

*7, place de Fontenay*
*75700 Paris*
*France*

## 2. TALK ABOUT THE PROBLEM

Talk to everyone—your parents and relatives, your neighbors, your friends, and your teachers—about what you're learning of illiteracy. Warn them of the dangers it holds not only for our own country but also the entire world. Tell them of the work that is being done to eradicate it, and point out that the struggle against illiteracy is an uphill one that needs the attention of all people, no matter their age.

You can also urge others to begin talking. There's nothing to stop you from asking your local newspaper and radio and television stations to provide information on the problem.

## 3. TAKE ACTION AT SCHOOL

At school, you can do far more than talk about the problem. For example, by yourself or with some of your friends, you could present a classroom program on illiteracy. The same program could then be presented at a school assembly. And you could get in touch with several local civic organizations, such as the Rotary and Kiwanis clubs, to see if they would be interested in having you present the program at one of their meetings. You also might want to form a club at school to study and discuss illiteracy.

## 4. BECOME A VOLUNTEER

As you know from reading chapter 7, there are many volunteer programs, from the local to the national level, dedicated to helping the illiterate learn to read and write. Ask your local library to point out the volunteer programs in your area. Or find out if your school sponsors a peer program. There is also a national organization that can provide you with information on local programs across the country, Contact Center. The Center's address is: P.O. Box 81826, Lincoln, Nebraska, 68501.

If you wish, you may call the Center on its national toll-free hot-line number and ask for information on the literacy program nearest your home. The number is: 800-228-8813.

Once you've located the program in your area, volunteer to work with it and take the training that will enable you to participate. If you don't wish to become an instructor, there are other jobs you can fill. The programs need volunteers to do clerical work, assist with publications (such as brochures and newsletters), answer telephones, and provide transportation for students without cars of their own. Working in any way possible to help a person learn to read and write is assuredly one of life's most satisfying jobs—and certainly one of its most valuable.

## 5. TAKE ACTION AT HOME

One of your most important anti-illiteracy actions can be taken at home. Do you have a little brother or sister, let's say a sister named Sally, who is in the first grade and is having a difficult time learning to read? You can help her become literate simply by reading aloud to her on a regular basis, perhaps each night before she goes to bed, and following a few simple rules as you do so. They are rules that you can later put to use when you have children of your own.

*To begin, choose a book with lots of pictures and few words. Better yet, let Sally select the book so that you're sure it's one she likes that interests her. You may find that she'll very often pick out the same book. But don't worry. There will be enough words in it for her to learn. As time goes on, there will be more and more books that interest her.*

*Children do a better job of learning to read when they become personally involved in what is happening on the page. And so, as you read aloud, encourage Sally to join in by asking her questions about the pictures, such as "Who is that?" and "What is that?" When she replies, you can help her become more involved by asking other questions: "What is Tom doing?" or "How fast do you think that car can go?"*

*When she gives a correct answer, repeat what she has said and praise her. This encourages her to go on reading and learning. But suppose you ask her to identify a word—perhaps* house*—and she gives an incorrect answer or doesn't know the answer. Don't frown or scold. Rather, say "That word is* house*. Can you say* house*?" or "Can you find* house *somewhere else on the page?"*

*Keep an eye out for the things in the story that interest Sally. Stop reading and listen to her when she talks about them. Then the two of you should talk them over. Here, you should do more listening than talking, always encouraging her to go on speaking.*

*At all times, praise her and, at all times, have fun as you're reading, listening, and talking. Do all you can to make the experience of learning to read pleasurable for Sally.*

The above rules are based on methods of teaching reading at home that are advised by Grover Whitehurst of the State University of New York.[1]

In the mid-1980s, Richard Anderson of the Center for the Study of Reading at the University of Illinois conducted a nationwide reading study of children from kindergarten through the sixth grade. The study found that the children whose parents read to them at home ended up being better readers, having better vocabularies, and being better able to understand a teacher's instructions.[2]

There is yet another way in which you can help Sally. Encourage her not only to read but also to write. It has long been known that the development of reading skills can be speeded up by writing activities that are started at a very early age. You need not make Sally's writing instruction difficult. Make a simple game of it instead, one that will easily bring success. You can start with having Sally copy a word here and there in a story. Then you can go on to having her (with your help) write the answers to simple questions, such as "What is the color of your dress? . . . What is the color of my eyes . . . Dad's hair . . . Mother's shoes?" Later, as her skill grows, you can ask her to write about what she sees in a picture or out in the backyard.

## 6. KEEP YOUR INTEREST UP FROM NOW ON

This is perhaps the most important of the six rules. Your current interest in the illiteracy problem can bring actions that will bear great fruit. But it is vital that you do not lose interest in it as time goes on but carry your present enthusiasm into your adulthood. Then you'll be able to do even greater work than you are now doing—with your own children, your community, your country, and the world.

Always remember that illiteracy will probably remain with the world for years to come. Every person who drops out of the battle will enable the problem to linger for a longer and longer time. Every person who sticks to the battle will help to shorten that time, at last reducing it to a matter of months, weeks, days, and finally hours.

# SOURCE NOTES

**Chapter One:**
**Illiteracy in America**

1. The stories of "Dan" and "Lora" are developed from interviews with two teenagers. The names are fictitious, as the young people do not wish their identities revealed.

2. The material explaining total and functional illiteracy is developed from: J-P Velis, "Waste," *UNESCO*, a publication of the United Nations Educational, Scientific, and Cultural Organization (July 1990): 31; "USA: The Problem in Our Country," *The Newsletter of the International Task Force on Literacy* (ITFL) (October 1990): 1.

3. The material in the section "Types of Illiteracy" is developed from: an interview with "Antonio," an Italian teenager who does not wish his real name used; D. and B. Bjorklund, "Babe Ruth Is Not a Candy Bar," *Parents* (September 1988): 127; J. P. Comer, MD, "Ignorance Is Not Bliss," *Parents* (March 1991): 193.

4. The material in the section "Illiteracy in the United States" is developed from: M. Halstuk, "Adults Who Can't Read Face Challenge of Illiteracy, *San Francisco Chronicle*, September 5, 1992; M. B. Zuckerman, "The Illiteracy Epidemic," *U.S. News & World Report*, June 12, 1989, 72; *Newsletter* (ITFL) (October 1990): 1; *Literacy Questions and Answers: General Facts*, an information publication by Contact Center, Lincoln, Nebraska, no publication date or page number given; Velis, 31.

5. The material in the section "Illiteracy Worldwide" is developed from: *1990: International Literacy Year*, an informational document by the United Nations Educational, Scientific, and Cultural Organization, June 1989, 1–5; and the following articles from *UNESCO*, a publication of the United Nations Educational, Scientific, and Cultural Organization, July 1990—S. Lourie, "World Literacy: Where We Stand Today," 1–2; J. Ryan, "From Rhetoric to Reality," 11.

6. The material in the section "The Costs of Illiteracy" is developed from: J. Chancellor, commentary on the costs of illiteracy, NBC Nightly News, July 21, 1991, transcript page 7; R. Tunley, "America's Secret Shame," *Reader's Digest* (September 1985): 104; B. Ward, "Literacy Now," *Sky* (April 1992): 24; Ryan, 12; *The Universal Almanac, 1992* (Kansas City: Andrews and McMeel, Universal Press Syndicate, 1991), 388.

7. *Literacy Questions and Answers*, no publication date or page number given; *1990: International Literacy Year*, 8.

**Chapter Two:**
**The Rise and Fall of Literacy in the United States**
1. The material in the section "Illiteracy in Early America" is developed from: T. A. Bailey, *The Ameri-*

can *Pageant: A History of the Republic* (Boston: D. C. Heath, 1956), 23, 77; M. Burke, *United States History: The Growth of Our Land* (Chicago: American Technical Society, 1957), 26–27, 223; "The American Experience: Education," *The Random House Encyclopedia*, 3rd Edition (New York: Random House, 1990), 1406.

2. The material in the section "The Beginnings of a School System in America" is developed from: H. B. Wilder, R. P. Ludlum, H. M. Brown, *This is America's Story*, 3rd Edition (Boston: Houghton Mifflin, 1966), 332; C. C. Calkins, editor, *The Story of America* (Pleasantville, New York: Reader's Digest Association, 1975), 128; G. V. D. and J. V. D. Southworth, *American History* (New York: Iroquois Publishing, 1934), 21, 83, 147.

3. The material in the section "The Nineteenth Century" is developed from : J. D. Hicks, *The Federal Union: A History of the United States to 1865*, 2nd Edition (Boston: Houghton Mifflin, 1952), 441–42; S. E. Morison and H. S. Commager, *The Growth of the American Republic* (New York: Oxford University Press, 1950), 288; Bailey, 338; Calkins, 127, 131–32, 321, 330, 431, 433; Southworth, 249; *The Encyclopedia of American Facts and Dates* (New York: Harper & Row, 1987), 23–24, 103, 357; *The World Almanac and Book of Facts, 1990* (New York: Pharos Books, 1989), 190, 191, 198; *The Universal Almanac, 1992* (Kansas City: Andrews and McMeel, Universal Press Syndicate, 1991), 201, 216; *The Random House Encyclopedia*, 1238, 2376.

4. The material in the section "The Twentieth Century" is developed from: J. Kozol, *Illiterate America* (New York: New American Library, 1986), 18, 37–38; L. Harris and Associates, "Poll on Young People's Skills," *San Francisco Chronicle*, September 30, 1991; Calkins, 135; The National Commission on

Excellence in Education, *A Nation at Risk: The Imperative for Educational Reform* (Washington, D.C.: U.S. Government Printing Office, 1983), 9; *The 1990 Information Please Almanac* (New York: Houghton Mifflin, 1989), 790; *Encyclopedia of American Facts and Dates*, 416, 419, 485, 565, 751, 753; *Universal Almanac*, 201.

## Chapter Three:
## Why Illiteracy: Classrooms and Conveniences

1. The material in the section "The Classroom" is developed from: E. Bowen, "Losing the War of Letters," *Time*, May 5, 1986, 68; J. D. Horan, *The Desperate Years* (New York: Bonanza Books, 1962), 133; Time-Life Editors, *This Fabulous Century: 1940–1950* (New York: Time-Life Books, 1969), 217; J. Silber, *Shooting Straight: What's Wrong with America and How to Fix It* (New York: Harper & Row, 1989), 6–7; C. C. Walcutt, editor, *Tomorrow's Illiterates* (Boston: Little Brown, 1961), 93–94; *Collier's Encyclopedia*, 3rd Edition (New York: Macmillan Educational Company, 1990), 110, 608; remarks by parents who do not wish to be identified.

2. The material in the section "The Electronic Age" is developed from: A. Atkins, "TV in the Classroom: Will Television as Teacher Harm Our School Kids?" *Better Homes & Gardens* (October 1990): 34, 36; S. Fritz et al, "Save Our Schools," *Omni* (April 1990): 46; J. W. Gardner, *Excellence: Can We Be Equal and Excellent Too?* (New York: Harper & Row, 1961), 89–90; P. Iyer, "History? Education? Zap! Pow! Cut!" *Time*, May 14, 1990, 98; Silber, 69–70.

## Chapter Four
## Why Illiteracy: Social Problems

1. The material in the section "Immigration" is developed from: E. Bowen, "Losing the War of Letters,"

*Time*, May 5, 1986, 68; L. Chavez, "Why Bilingual Education Fails Hispanic Children, *McCall's* (March 1991): 59–60; R. G. McLeod and T. Schreiner, "One in 11 Have Trouble Speaking California's Official Language," *San Francisco Chronicle*, May 12, 1992; C. Leslie, D. Glick, and J. Gordon, "Classrooms of Babel," *Newsweek*, February 11, 1991, 56–57; P. Noonan, "Why the World Comes Here," *Reader's Digest* (July 1991): 42; J. Pinchot, *The Mexicans in America* (Minneapolis: Lerner Publishing, 1989), 54–59; "Immigration," *The Universal Almanac, 1992* (Kansas City: Andrews and McMeel, Universal Press Syndicate, 1991), 216.

2. The material in the section "Poverty" is developed from: N. J. Perry, "The Education Crisis: What Business Can Do," *Fortune*, July 4, 1988, 71; J. Sepulveda-Bailey, "The Challenge of Migrant Education," *Hispanic*, April 29, 1989, 66; J. Silber, *Shooting Straight: What's Wrong with America and How to Fix It* (New York: Harper & Row, 1989), 30–31; "The Homeless," *Universal Almanac*, 214–15; "Senator Byrd Hints U.S. Should Cut Influx of Non-English Speakers," *San Francisco Chronicle* (from Associated Press), June 26, 1992; the story of the homeless child, "Rose Marie," is told by her mother, who wishes that neither she nor her child be identified; the description of classroom behavior in a poor Los Angeles area is from an interview with a teacher who wishes to remain anonymous.

3. The material in the section "Reverse Problems" is developed from: American Health Magazine Service, "Working Teens Have More Problems," *San Francisco Chronicle*, July 7, 1992; J. W. Gardner, *Excellence: Can We Be Equal and Excellent Too?* (New York: Harper & Row, 1961), 93, 94; National Commission on Excellence, *A Nation at Risk: The Imperative for Educational Reform* (Washington, D.C.: U.S. Government Printing Office, 1983), 12, 18–19.

**Chapter Five**
**Fighting Illiteracy: The United States**

1. The material in the section "The Federal Government" is developed from: N. Asimov, "Bush to Announce Plan for $1000 School Vouchers," *San Francisco Chronicle*, June 25, 1992; D. Brady, "Reinventing School," *Maclean's*, April 29, 1991, 50; H. Fields, "Bush Education Plan Skimps on New Funding," *Publishers Weekly*, May 3, 1991; H. Fields, "Literacy Bill Progresses with Senate's Okay," *Publishers Weekly*, July 19, 1991, 6; D. Sarasohn, "Time Is Running Out for Bush to Be Education President," *San Francisco Chronicle*, September 8, 1991; B. Ward, "Literacy Now," *Sky* (April 1992): 24–25; W. Shapiro, "Tough Choice," *Time*, September 16, 1991, 54–55; "Bush Focuses on Education," *San Francisco Chronicle* (from *New York Times*), September 4, 1991.

2. The material in the section "The States and Their Local School Districts" is developed from: S. Allis, "Why 180 Days Aren't Enough," *Time*, September 2, 1991, 64–65; S. Barrington, "Year-Round Schooling Has Healthy Bottom Line," *The Province*, August 22, 1991; M. Jordan, "The Move Toward a Longer School Year," *San Francisco Chronicle* (from *Washington Post*), March 22, 1992; S. Tifft, "How to Tackle School Reform," *Time*, August 4, 1992, 46–47; "Schools Pay Kids to Read," *San Francisco Chronicle* (from *Los Angeles Times*), August 7, 1992; information supplied by the State Department of Education, Arkansas.

3. The material in the section "American Business" is developed from: S. Fritz, D. Sobel, J. K. Hefner, R. Fleming, and J. Cummings, "Save Our Schools," *Omni* (April 1990): 42, 43, 96–100; J. Kozol, *Illiterate America* (New York: New American Library, 1986), 18–19, 81–86; N. J. Perry, "The Education Crisis: What Business Can Do," *Fortune*, July 4, 1988, 71–76; "My Friends Are Killing Each Other," *Fortune*, July 4, 1988, 80.

## Chapter Six
## Fighting Illiteracy: The World

1. The material in the section "At the International Level" is developed from: J. Ryan, "From Rhetoric to Reality," *UNESCO*, a publication of the United Nations Educational, Scientific, and Cultural Organization, July 1990, 10–11; *1990: International Literacy Year*, an informational document by the United Nations Educational, Scientific, and Cultural Organization, June 1989, 1–5; and the following articles in *UN Chronicle*, March 1990—"Educating All: Everyone Has the Right to an Education," 58; "Illiteracy Knows No Borders," 59; "Launching the Possible Dream," 49–51.

2. The material in the section "At the National Level" is developed from: C. Jeffries, *Illiteracy: A World Problem* (New York: Praeger, 1967), 66–68; H. L. Mathews, *Revolution in Cuba* (New York: Charles Scribner's Sons, 1975), 181–84; the following articles in *UN Chronicle*, March 1990—"Launching the Possible Dream," 50–51; "Literacy on the Home Front," 52–53.

3. The material in the section "The World: Women and Illiteracy" is developed from: A. Lind, "The Gender Gap," *UNESCO*, a publication of the United Nations Educational, Scientific, and Cultural Organization (March 1990): 24–26; "Closing the Gender Gap: Literacy for Women and Girls," *UN Chronicle* (March 1990): 56–57; "Women Are Poorer," *UN Chronicle* (September 1990): 47.


## Chapter Seven
## Fighting Illiteracy: Programs and Volunteers

1. J. Kozol, *Illiterate America* (New York: New American Library, 1986), 41.

2. "Germaine's" story was told to co-author M. M. Scariano by a student member of Mrs. Scariano's recent General Education Diploma classes.

3. "Joe's" story also comes from a member of co-author Scariano's General Education Diploma classes.
4. Ibid.
5. The material in the section "Laubach Literacy Action" is developed from: C. Jeffries, *Illiteracy: A World Problem* (New York: Praeger, 1967), 37–40, 107–9, 111, 113; two publications by Contact Center, Lincoln, Nebraska—*Literacy Questions and Answers: General Facts* and *Literacy Questions and Answers: Volunteering*, no publication date or page numbers given.
6. The material in the section "Literacy Volunteers of America" is developed from: W. Anderson, *Read with Me* (Boston: Houghton Mifflin, 1990), 42–47, 65, 85; *Literacy Questions and Answers: Volunteering*, no publication date or page number given.
7. The material in the section "Local Programs and Volunteers" is developed from: Anderson, 95; "Our Times: A Monthly Report on the State of the Culture," *Life*, July 1992, 23; *Literacy Questions and Answers: Volunteering*, no publication date or page number given; personal knowledge of co-author Scariano.

**Chapter Eight**
**Joining the Battle**

1. "How to Read to Your Child," *Parade Magazine*, May 10, 1992, 17.
2. R. L. Gould, "Read Me a Story," *Parade Magazine*, May 10, 1992, 16.

# BIBLIOGRAPHY

**Books**

Anderson, Walter. *Read with Me*. Boston: Houghton Mifflin, 1990.

Bailey, Thomas A. *The American Pageant: A History of the Republic*. Boston: D. C. Heath, 1956.

Blumenfeld, Samuel L. *The New Illiterates*. New Rochelle, N.Y.: Arlington House, 1973.

Burke, Merle. *United States History: The Growth of Our Land*. Chicago: American Technical Society, 1957.

Calkins, Charles C., ed. *The Story of America*. Pleasantville, N.Y.: Reader's Digest Association, 1975.

Carruth, Gorton. *The Encyclopedia of American Facts & Dates*. 8th Edition. New York: Harper & Row, 1987.

Cooke, Alistair. *Alistair Cooke's America*. New York: Knopf, 1973.

Gardner, John W. *Excellence: Can We Be Equal and Excellent Too?*. New York: Harper & Row, 1961.

Hicks, John D. *The Federal Union: A History of the United States to 1865*. 2nd Edition. Boston: Houghton Mifflin, 1952.

Hoffman, Mark S., ed. *The World Almanac and Book of Facts, 1990*. New York: Pharos Books, 1989.

Holdaway, Don. *Stability and Change in Literacy Learning*. Portsmouth, N.H.: Heinemann Educational Books, 1988.

Horan, James D. *The Desperate Years*. New York: Bonanza Books, 1962.

Johnston, Bernard, ed. *Collier's Encyclopedia*. New York and London: MacMillan Educational Company, P. F. Colliers Inc., 1990.

Kozol, Jonathan. *Illiterate America*. New York: New American Library, 1986.

————*Prisoners of Silence*. New York: Continuum Publishing, 1980.

Jeffries, Sir Charles. *Illiteracy: A World Problem*. New York: Praeger, 1967.

Johnson, Otto, ed. *The 1990 Information Please Almanac*. New York: Houghton Mifflin, 1989.

Long, Robert Emmet, ed. *The State of U.S. Education*. New York: H. W. Wilson, 1991.

Mathews, Herbert L. *Revolution in Cuba*. New York: Charles Scribner's Sons, 1975.

Mitchell, James, ed. *The Random House Encyclopedia*. 3rd Edition. New York: Random House, 1990.

Morison, Samuel E., and Henry S. Commager. *The Growth of the American Republic*. New York: Oxford University Press, 1950.

Muzzey, David Saville. *A History of Our Country*. Boston: Ginn, 1941.

Pinchot, Jane. *The Mexicans in America*. Minneapolis, Minn.: Lerner Publishing, 1989.

Prete, Barbara, and Gary E. Strong, eds. *Literate America Emerging*. Sacramento, Calif.: California State Library Foundation, 1991.

Silber, John. *Shooting Straight: What's Wrong with America and How to Fix It.* New York: Harper & Row, 1989.

Time-Life Editors. *This Fabulous Century, 1940–1950.* New York: Time-Life Books, 1969.

Walcutt, Charles C., ed. *Tomorrow's Illiterates.* Boston: Little Brown, 1961.

Wilder, Howard Baker, Robert P. Ludlum, and Harriett McCune Brown. *This Is America's Story.* 3rd Edition. Boston: Houghton Mifflin, 1966.

Wright, John W., ed. *The Universal Almanac, 1992.* Kansas City: Andrews and McMeel, Universal Press Syndicate, 1991.

**Magazines**

Allis, Sam. "Why 180 Days Aren't Enough." *Time,* September 2, 1991.

————"George Bush's Point Man." *Time,* September 16, 1991.

Atkins, Andrea. "TV in the Classroom: Will Television as Teacher Harm Our School Kids?" *Better Homes and Gardens,* October 1990.

Blodgett, Bonnie. "The Private Hell of Public Education." *Lear's,* April 1992.

Bowen, Ezra. "Losing the War of Letters." *Time,* May 5, 1986.

Brady, Diane. "Reinventing School: George Bush Pledges Better Education." *Maclean's,* April 29, 1991.

Bjorklund, David, and Barbara Bjorklund. "Babe Ruth Is Not a Candy Bar—and Other Facts Children Must Know to Boost Their Learning Power." *Parents,* September 1988.

Chavez, Linda. "Why Bilingual Education Fails Hispanic Children." *McCall's,* March 1991.

Comer, James P., M.D. "Ignorance Is Not Bliss." *Parents,* March 1991.

Fields, Howard, "Barbara Bush Foundation for Family

Literacy Launched at White House." *Publishers Weekly*, March 24, 1989.

———. "Bush Education Plan Skimps on New Funding." *Publishers Weekly*, May 3, 1991.

———. "Literacy Bill Progresses with Senate's Okay." *Publishers Weekly*, July 19, 1991.

———. "$1.1 Billion Literacy Spending Bill Becomes Law." *Publishers Weekly*, August 16, 1991.

———. "Education Finds U.S. Reading, Writing Skills Worsen." *Publishers Weekly*, November 8, 1991.

Fritz, Sandy, Dava Sobel, J. Keith Hefner, Robert Fleming, and John Cummings. "Save Our Schools." *Omni*, April 1990.

Gould, Randi Londer. "Read Me a Story." *Parade Magazine*, May 10, 1992.

Henry, Sarah. "English Only: The Language of Discrimination." *Hispanic*, March 1990.

Iyer, Pico. "History? Education? Zap! Pow! Cut!" *Time*, May 14, 1990.

Keizer, Gregg. "Class Acts." *Omni*, December 1991.

Leslie, Connie, Daniel Glick, and Jeanne Gordon. "Classrooms of Babel." *Newsweek*, February 11, 1991.

*Life.* "A Centenarian and a Grad Find That New Beginnings Come at Any Age" (featured in "Our Times: A Monthly Report on the State of the Culture"). July 1992.

Lipson, Eden Ross. "Reading Along with Barbara Bush: The Endings Are Mostly Happy." *New York Times*, May 21, 1989.

Manley, Dexter. "Until He Tackled His Illiteracy, the Redskins' Gridiron Terror Lived in Fear of the ABC's." *People Weekly*, September 25, 1989.

Morey, Janet Robbie. "Don't Take Me Off Your Heart." *Reader's Digest*, February 1991.

*Newsweek.* "Give Me Your Smart, Your Skilled . . ." December 17, 1990.

Noonan, Peggy. "Why the World Comes Here." *Reader's Digest*, July 1991.

Packard, Vance. "Are We Becoming a Nation of Illiterates?" *Reader's Digest*. April 1974.

Perry, Nancy J. "The Education Crisis: What Business Can Do." *Fortune*, July 4, 1988.

Ryan, Michael. "Where Parents and Child Learn Together." *Parade Magazine*, July 12, 1992.

Sepulveda-Bailey, Jaime. "The Challenge of Migrant Education." *Hispanic*, April 1989.

Shapiro, Walter. "Tough Choice." *Time*, September 16, 1991.

Summer, Bob. "Atlanta Holds a Book Festival to Benefit Adult Literacy." *Publishers Weekly*, May 10, 1991.

Tifft, Susan. "How to Tackle School Reform: Three States Rise to the Challenge and Provide Valuable Lessons." *Time*, August 14, 1992.

*Time*. "What Does a Stomach Do?" September 30, 1991.

Toch, Thomas, and Jerry Buckley. "The Blackboard Jumble: After the Riots, the Presidential Candidates Focus on Fixing Schools." *U.S. News & World Report*, May 25, 1992.

Tucker, William. "Foot in the Door." *Forbes*, February 3, 1992.

Tunley, Roul. "America's Secret Shame." *Reader's Digest*, September 1985.

*U.S. News & World Report*. "What SAT Scores Don't Tell." September 9, 1991.

Ward, Bernie. "Literacy Now." *Sky*, April 1992.

Zuckerman, Mortimer B. "The Illiteracy Epidemic." *U.S. News & World Report*, June 12, 1989.

**Newspapers**

American Health Magazine Service. "Working Teens Have More Problems." *San Francisco Chronicle*, July 7, 1992.

Asimov, Nanette. "Bush to Announce Plan for $1000

School Vouchers." *San Francisco Chronicle*, June 25, 1992.

———. "S. F. Schools Criticized on Teaching of Minorities." *San Francisco Chronicle*, June 27, 1992.

Associated Press. "U.S. Drops to Fifth Place in Competitiveness. *San Francisco Chronicle*, June 26, 1992.

Barrington, Stephen. "Graduate Literacy Tests Urged." *The Province* (Vancouver, B.C.), August 22, 1991.

———. "Year-Round Schooling Has Healthy Bottom Line." *The Province*, August 22, 1991/

De Witt, Karen. "Labor Dept. Outlines Job Skills Students Will Need in Future." *New York Times*, July 3, 1991.

Farney, Dennis. "Can Big Money Fix Urban School Systems? A Test Is Under Way." *Wall Street Journal*, January 7, 1992.

Griffin, Susan. "Potential Dropouts Helped." *The Province*, August 22, 1991.

———. "Problem of Adult Illiterates Helped by Special Programs." *The Province*, August 22, 1991.

Halstuk, Martin. "Adults Who Can't Read Face Challenge of Illiteracy." *San Francisco Chronicle*, September 5, 1992.

Lou Harris and Associates. "Poll on Young People's Skills." *San Francisco Chronicle*, September 30, 1991.

Jordan, Mary. "The Move Toward a Longer School Year." *San Francisco Chronicle* (from *Washington Post*), March 29, 1992.

Lewthwaite, Gilbert A. "The Men's Decade: Educated Males to be in Demand." *San Francisco Chronicle* (from *Baltimore Sun*), March 2, 1992.

McLeod, Ramon G., and Tim Schreiner. "One in 11 Have Trouble Speaking California's Official Language." *San Francisco Chronicle*, May 13, 1992.

Pender, Kathleen. "School Crisis Alarms Business." *San Francisco Chronicle*, September 28, 1992.

———. "A Look at Schools with Business Eyes." *San Francisco Chronicle*, September 28, 1992.

Putka, Gary. "Concern Goes Up as SAT Scores Go Down," *Wall Street Journal*, August 27, 1991.

Robinson, Herb. "Your Sentence Is to Read This Sentence." *Seattle Times*, September 20, 1991.

"School Stress and Success in Japan." *San Francisco Examiner*, May 3, 1992.

"Schools Pay Kids to Read." *San Francisco Chronicle* (from *Los Angeles Times*), August 7, 1992.

Stout, Hilary. "Students Fail to Reach Level Set in U.S. Plan." *Wall Street Journal*, October 1, 1991.

Woltman, Julia. "Study Cites 32 Programs as Effective in Boosting Literacy." *Education Week*, April 20, 1988.

Yates, Ronald E. "U.S. Not the Swiftest in the Race to Compete." *San Francisco Examiner* (from *Chicago Tribune*), July 5, 1992.

## Organizational Publications

Center for Early Adolescence. "Curriculum and Instruction." *Common Focus*, Volume 8, Number 1, 1987.

————. "Project on Adolescent Literacy: Update." *Common Focus*, Volume 9, Number 1, 1989.

Contact Center. *Literacy Questions & Answers: General Facts*. No publication date given.

————. *Literacy Questions and Answers: Volunteering*. No publication date given.

International Task Force on Literacy. "USA: The Problem in Our Country." *The Newsletter of the International Task Force on Literacy*, October 1990.

Lind, Agneta. "The Gender Gap." *UNESCO*, July 1990.

Lourie, Sylvain. "World Literacy: Where We Stand Today." *UNESCO*, July 1990.

Ryan, John. "From Rhetoric to Reality." *UNESCO*, July 1990.

United Nations. "Educating All: Everyone Has the Right to an Education." *UN Chronicle*, March 1990.

————. "Illiteracy Knows No Borders." *UN Chronicle*, March 1990.

———. "Launching the Possible Dream." *UN Chronicle*, March 1990.

———. "Literacy on the Home Front." *UN Chronicle*, March 1990.

———. "How Is Literacy Taught?" *UN Chronicle*, March 1990.

———. "Closing the Gender Gap: Literacy for Women and Girls." *UN Chronicle*, March 1990.

———. "Women Are Poorer." *UN Chronicle*, September 1990.

United Nations Educational, Scientific, and Cultural Organization. *1990 International Literacy Year: A Time for Action.* No publication date given.

**Report**

National Commission on Excellence in Education. *A Nation at Risk: The Imperative for Educational Reform.* Washington, D.C.: U. S. Government Printing Office, 1983.

**Television Transcript**

National Broadcasting Company. *NBC Nightly News.* July 25, 1991.

# INDEX